SEWING

ANTON
SANDQVIST

MAKING BACKPACKS
AND OTHER STUFF

HEAVY-DUTY SEWING

FRANCES LINCOLN

**The measurements in this
book are given in metric.**

1 mm = 3/64 inch	1 cm = 25/64 inch	10 cm = 3 15/16 inch	1 m = 3 ft 3 inch
2 mm = 5/64 inch	2 cm = 25/32 inch	20 cm = 7 7/8 inch	2 m = 6 ft 7 inch
3 mm = 1/8 inch	3 cm = 1 3/16 inch	30 cm = 11 13/16 inch	3 m = 9 ft 10 inch
4 mm = 5/32 inch	4 cm = 1 37/64 inch	40 cm = 15 3/4 inch	
5 mm = 13/64 inch	5 cm = 1 31/32 inch	50 cm = 19 11/16 inch	
6 mm = 15/64 inch	6 cm = 2 23/64 inch	60 cm = 23 5/8 inch	
7 mm = 9/32 inch	7 cm = 2 3/4 inch	70 cm = 27 9/16 inch	
8 mm = 5/16 inch	8 cm = 3 5/32 inch	80 cm = 31 1/2 inch	
9 mm = 23/64 inch	9 cm = 3 35/64 inch	90 cm = 35 7/16 inch	

INTRODUCTION

Heavy-duty sewing is about using a needle and thread, a sewing machine and sturdy fabrics, to make practical and hardwearing everyday items like backpacks, bags and knife pouches. Compared to clothes, the needlework is less complicated – straight stitch, for the most part – and the construction is both simpler and more attractive than in many shop-bought products, which also makes the items easier to repair if they wear out or break.

The challenge in heavy-duty sewing actually lies in the quality of the material; you might find yourself working with numerous layers of sturdy fabric, and it can be tricky to bring the pieces to together in a neat, durable way using an ordinary sewing machine. But, if you take things slowly, and with a little bit of patience, you'll be able to produce good, individual results with character.

Many of the techniques I'll talk about here are things I've learnt through years of trial and error; I'm by no means a pro. It's like most things in life: practice makes perfect. I started sewing objects of my own during the 1980s, when I was a teenager. To begin with, I mostly stuck to adjusting my jeans, but I later started making my own outdoor items from scratch. A couple of earlier projects which I remember particularly clearly are a pair of moss green fleece trousers with ripstop reinforcements, and a kind of pouch with straps which transformed an inflatable underlay into a chair. This was in the early 90s, when I was doing a lot of climbing, and many of my climbing friends also sewed. One of them had even made a portaledge, a kind of tent you hang from a couple of anchor points on a vertical rock face when you need to sleep on a big climb. So, you see, it's possible to sew most things yourself. In this book, however, we'll be sticking to much simpler and far less life-sustaining items.

The projects featured in this book are designed to be used in a number of different environments, from the forest to the city and everywhere in between. I like to spend my free time outdoors, tinkering about with my motorbike and taking it out on the road, and this is reflected in the selection. My interest in nature is responsible for many of the best items I've produced over the years. One of my favourite pastimes during the winter is cross-country skiing on loose snow. It's hard work, but you glide almost silently through the forest and it's a great workout away from the treadmill. You also get to see a whole load of animals and beautiful scenery, plus there's a lot of stopping for coffee. For this hobby, I've designed a day backpack (page 52) and a pair of gaiters (page 66) to stop the snow from getting into my boots. For motorbike rides, I've made a duffel bag (page 92) that's perfect strapped to the sissy bar when I'm going on a long trip. That said, I've also sewn plenty of things for the home. One particular favourite is the simple, beautiful hanging flowerpot (page 104) for growing herbs in. I hope you'll see these projects as a source of inspiration and feel that you can develop or adapt them in line with your particular needs.

In addition to the projects, the book goes through working methods, equipment and materials. This is where I share my self-taught (but hopefully still useful) knowledge of heavy-duty sewing. I'll talk about subjects like construction and stitches, as well as different types of material suitable for projects like this, their qualities and where you can get hold of them. And I'll mention the equipment, that's always popular. Sewing machines are fascinating objects, an incredible invention that has saved people an enormous amount of time. I'll describe the basic functions of a sewing machine and explain how to set it up correctly so that you, as a beginner, have all the knowledge you need to be able to buy your own and get to work.

One particularly relevant aspect of home sewing, other than being really fun, is that you can actually *produce* the things you need, rather than buying them. It means slightly less consumption, and you can't get any more local. Buying a sewing machine may mean a substantial investment, but you'll come to see that it's worth every penny. Aside from being able to work on projects of your own, you'll also be able to repair things. For families with small children, in particular, I think that a sewing machine is essential. I repair my own and my children's clothes and am able to drastically increase their longevity as a result. If you can manage a few of the projects in this book, you can repair things at home – that's an additional bonus.

Before you get started, my advice to you is as follows: read some of the theory, but not too much that you hamper your creativity, and then get to work on one of the projects. It's best to solve any problems as and when they crop up. After you've worked on a couple of projects, you'll have a much better sense of what is what, you'll be able to work out what you need and want to sew, and then just do it.

With this book, my aim is ultimately to share a bit of enthusiasm, inspiration, knowledge and advice so that you can create your own functional products. It isn't difficult, it just takes a little patience and a pinch of care. It's so much fun – you can really switch off and focus on what you're sewing. And you'll also end up with some really great items. Welcome to heavy-duty sewing!

THEORY

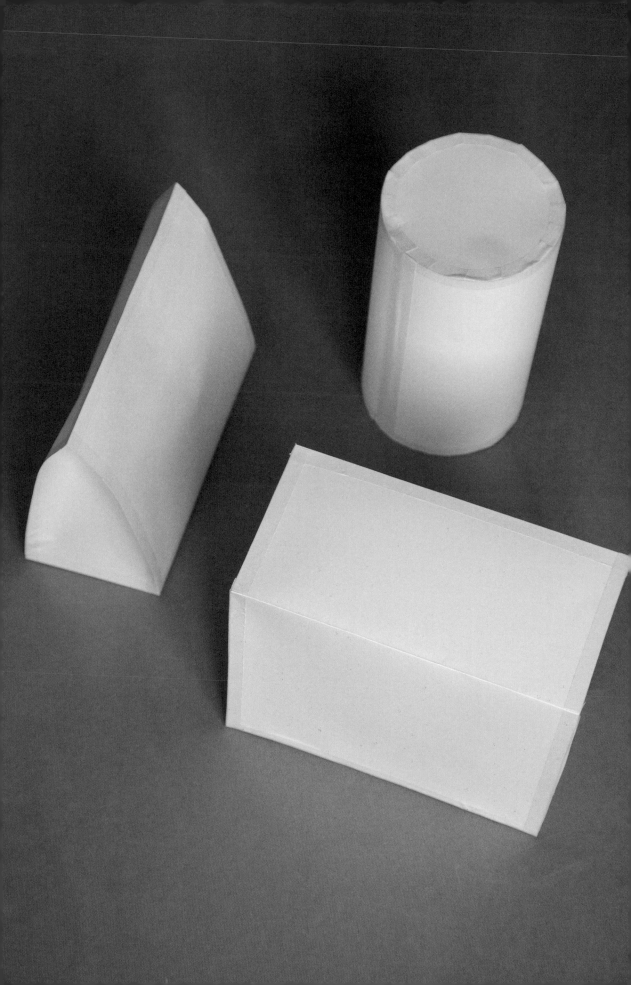

CONSTRUCTION

Construction in sewing is about understanding and describing how the item you are planning to sew is structured, which parts go into making it, and how these come together to create a functioning product. Textile designs can be very complex, with many parts – just look at a suit, for example – but they can also be incredibly simple, as in a canvas tote. Creating advanced items is a complex area of knowledge; there are entire courses devoted to cutting and pattern making, so I won't be getting into that here. Instead, the focus of this book is on relatively simple everyday items. If you ask me, the simple solution with the fewest parts is often also the most attractive and durable.

When thinking about the construction of a textile product, it's about understanding how you can create a three-dimensional figure – an object with a volume – that also looks how you imagined it. A backpack is a good example. Backpacks can be made in a number of different ways; they can be square, cylindrical, or half pear-shaped, and they all form a geometric volume of some kind when filled. Add two shoulder straps and some kind of opening to allow access to this inner space, and you've made yourself a backpack. Some simple and practical geometric shapes that work well for backpacks include: cuboids, prisms and cylinders, or combinations of these. It's also quite common to give a few of the edges a different shape – you could use a cylinder where the base and top consist of flattened circles, for example, or squares with rounded corners or curves, or a cuboid where the front is curved inwards at the top and has rounded corners at the bottom. The best approach is to start with a simple geometric form and then tweak it to achieve the shape you want.

Rounded and organic forms are more difficult to create using material than angular ones, since the material itself is flat. Just look at a football. It consists of a large number of smaller pieces sewn together to build a sphere. The more pieces it is made up of, and the smaller they are, the more perfect the sphere. With a solid grasp of how to create a three-dimensional geometric shape using flat pieces of material, you can also come up with new varieties, change the format or size, combine different solutions and create completely individual constructions.

Paper models showing various possible shapes of a toiletry bag.

As an example and a simple thought exercise, I'll use the next page to show three different options for creating a toiletry bag, and I'll also discuss the advantages and disadvantages of each.

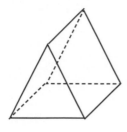

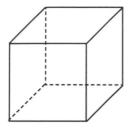

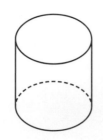

Toiletry bag in the shape of a triangular prism

A triangular toiletry bag has a zip at the top, and when this is opened the bag becomes a cuboid. It's relatively simple to sew, since the zip is added at the edge of two pieces of fabric, a simple kind of seam. The front piece, base and back piece can be made from one single piece of fabric, and the sides from two separate, rectangular pieces. These fold to become triangular when the zip is closed, but are rectangular when it is open. As a result, this particular construction has a smaller volume when closed than it does when open. It consists of few individual pieces and therefore has relatively few seams, which makes it quick to sew. It is a classic, attractive shape for a toiletry bag.

Toiletry bag in the shape of a cuboid

The construction of a cuboid is slightly more complicated since the zip is in the middle of a piece of fabric, but that isn't too difficult to master. This item can vary in shape depending on whether you choose straight or rounded corners. The cuboid bag can be sewn from just two pieces of material, or from six if you want to make things more difficult. It would also be possible, albeit slightly unconventional, to place the zip on one edge, or along three edges, so that it forms a lid.

Toiletry bag in the shape of a cylinder

A cylindrical bag looks good, but can be slightly impractical since any pockets on the inside will be difficult to reach. That said, a smaller variant makes a great pencil case. Like the cuboid, it is slightly harder to sew since the zip connects all three pieces of fabric and is sewn into place in the middle of the end pieces.

The formulas below show how to calculate the volume (in litres) of your design.

Volume = Base area × height

Base area (triangle) = (B × H)/2

Base area (rectangle) = B × H

Base area (circle) = (3.14 × D × D)/4

Use centimetre measures.

100 cm³ = 1 litre

A good method for checking that you're happy with shape and format before you start cutting your material is to make a paper model of your design. Doing so will give you a good idea of the proportions, and you can adjust the paper model until you're happy with the shape. You can then take it apart and use the pieces as patterns for cutting the fabric. Remember that a pattern piece from a paper model will need to be increased in size to allow for the seams on each edge (the seam allowance is the amount of extra material needed to be able to create a seam). Thin cardboard which is slightly thicker than ordinary printer paper (*c.* 150 gsm, for example) is suitable for making these models. 20–25 mm masking tape is recommended for sticking the pieces together.

Begin by deciding what size you want your project to be, i.e. the height × width × depth, and then work out how big the pieces of paper need to be. The simplest approach is to begin by cutting out the side pieces (the ends of a cylinder) at the right size, and then cut the main body so that it is slightly too big. Next, line up the main body with one of the side pieces, mark and cut away any excess. Then, all that's left is to tape the pieces together and decide whether that is the shape you wanted.

MATERIAL

The objects we use often, and which get a lot of wear need to be durable, and that places demands on both the stitching and the material. Choosing a hardwearing and suitably thick and stiff fabric is possibly the most important step in ending up with a good final product. For bags and similar, you need a relatively tough material which gives stability, but given that the majority of fabric shops tend to focus on clothing and curtains, this kind of fabric unfortunately isn't always that easy to get hold of. That said, you do still have options in ordinary fabric shops: upholstery canvas, sheeting, beaver nylon and poplin. Canvas sold by companies which produce boat covers and awnings can also work well. Whatever you can't find in a shop can always be tracked down and ordered online. At Etsy.com, for example, you can find most kinds of fabric, but sadly often from sellers outside the EU, meaning you may have to import it.

Fabric, or woven fabric as we'll stick to in this book, consists of fibres that have been spun to form threads, which are then woven together in various ways, to make fabric. Depending on the type of material the fibres are made of, how thick the threads are, and which weaving method has been used, the fabric produced will have different qualities: it might be soft and pliable, stiff and sturdy, thick or thin, dense or sparse, patterned or smooth.

The vertical threads in a weave (those kept taut in a classic loom) are called warp, and the threads pulled through the warp during the weaving process are called weft. If two different threads are used as warp and weft, the material may end up with a right side (front) and a wrong side (back). This is important when it comes to bringing the pieces of fabric together for sewing. Denim is a good example of a material that has a right side and a wrong side, since the warp is blue and the weft is white.

Different sturdy fabrics, i.e. with different deniers but woven in the same way: plain weave. From top: cotton/polyester poplin, c. 200 denier; canvas of the same material, c. 400 denier; nylon cordura at 500 denier, and cotton canvas at c. 1,000 denier.

Since woven textiles have a very long history and have been developed and used in parallel in many areas of the world, there are a number of different terms for fabrics, as well as ways to classify them:

➻ PPI (picks per inch) and EPI (ends per inch): The number of weft threads per inch, and the number of warp threads per inch – i.e. a measure of a material's density.

17

➤ DENIER: A unit of measure of the linear mass density of the fibres, which is a rough measure of the fibres' thickness. Warp and weft can have different thread thicknesses. A 1 denier thread weighs 1 gram per 9,000 metres.

➤ WEIGHT PER M^2 (gsm): The weight in grams of the fabric per m^2.

➤ OZ PER YARD^2: As above, but using the American measure of yards. 1 gsm = 1 oz./yd^2 × 33.9

For the outer material of bags, you need a relatively hardwearing and sturdy fabric. This is partly because the bag will be subjected to wear and tear and heavy loads, and partly because it helps the bag not to feel too sloppy. That said, the fabric also can't be too thick – a heavier material will produce a more robust bag, but it will also lead to a heavier bag. Thicker, more densely woven material is also more difficult to sew, given that you will often be sewing through between 2–6 layers at a time.

In addition to outer material, you will also need lining. Many shop-bought bags have a thin polyester lining, because the material is cheap and lightweight, but the shiny, slippery look it gives isn't so nice. It's better to use a slightly more heavy-duty lining containing a cotton mix instead, e.g. poplin.

A material weight between 280 and 510 gsm (c.8–15 oz./yd^2) is quite suitable as an outer material for a bag, and 100–250 gsm (c.3–7 oz./yd^2) works well for lining, internal pockets and other details where you want a slightly thinner, lighter material.

Water resistance is something else to consider. Watertight fabrics, which have a layer of polyurethane on the inside, are available. Waxed fabrics will also resist water for a while – and you can even wax your fabric yourself. A densely woven fabric is, naturally, more water resistant than a sparse one, so if you want to use cotton, choose a densely woven quality for greater water resistance.

Below is a description of some common types of weave which work well for heavy-duty projects:

➤ CANVAS is made using plain weave, where the threads are woven one over one, as per the image on the next page. Canvas is often woven using threads of cotton, linen or a mixture, i.e. cotton and polyester. Canvas is available in a number of different densities and weights, some of them very thick. The right and wrong side are usually identical.

➤ TWILL is another type of weave, has a visible 45 degree diagonal pattern on the surface. The pattern is formed through the way in which the threads are woven together: the interlacing points between the threads move one step to the side with each new thread. There are various ways of doing this, 2/1 and 3/1 among them. 2/1 means that two warp threads are crossed by the weft thread, and that the position of this moves one step to the side with each row. The denim used in jeans is a 3/1 twill where the warp is an indigo cotton and the weft is white or natural cotton thread. Twill is more resistant to tearing than canvas.

➤ CORDURA is a brand name for a collection of different materials with high durability. The weave was initially developed for military purposes, but nylon cordura is now a very common material in backpacks and bags, and even in protective clothing for bikers. Cordura is usually woven from nylon, but polyester is also available. The weaving technique is usually a 2–2 plain weave, basketweave or dobby weave (both of which are variants of plain weave), but ripstop is also possible.

➤ RIPSTOP is a type of weave in which thicker nylon threads are woven into the fabric at regular intervals. The purpose is as the name suggests: to stop ripping. If a small rip occurs, the strong nylon threads help to prevent it from growing.

➤ POPLIN, like canvas, is a plain weave where the warp and weft are the same thickness. However, unlike canvas, the warp in poplin is twice as dense as the weft, and the threads are thinner. Poplin is often made using cotton, but wool, silk, viscose and polyester are also possible. It is a common material in shirts, work wear and upholstery fabrics. It's difficult to tell a thin canvas from a thick poplin.

Weaving principles for plain weave and twill.

➤ JERSEY isn't used quite so often in heavy-duty projects, but knowing about it is useful all the same. Jersey is a machine-knitted fabric which is elastic precisely because it is knitted and not woven, like the fabrics mentioned above. It is used in t-shirts and underwear, for example. Cotton is the most common fibre used in jersey, but synthetic fibres are also common. To sew jersey, you need to use a specific type of sewing machine – a so-called overlocker machine.

PADDING MATERIALS

To create a padded back section for a backpack, or a protective bottom for a bag, we use different materials between the outer fabric and the lining. Sometimes, these materials are glued to the outer layer, and some-times they are left loose, being sewn into position between the layers. These materials are known as non-wovens. As padding, you could use a thin sleeping mat or some kind of foam. 2–5 mm is a suitable thickness. At the bottom of larger leather bags, and also in some fabric bags, you will sometimes find a stiff piece of cardboard. This isn't ordinary card-board, it is more durable and treated to tolerate more moisture. That often works well instead of sewing padding into the bottom.

THREAD

There are a number of different sewing threads available, in materials like polyester, cotton, flax, nylon, and mixtures of these. Well-stocked fabric shops or sewing machine specialists should be able to give you advice on the best thread to use. When sewing durable items, you need a strong thread. I use a fairly substantial polyester thread from Gütermann called Extra Strong M782. It's available in a relatively large number of colours and is sold in the majority of ordinary fabric shops. Gütermann Tera 40 is another good choice for heavy-duty projects. A needle size of 90–100 is suitable for these threads. Naturally, there are other thread brands which will work just as well.

To hand sew leather details, you'll need to use a rather thick, waxed thread made from linen or synthetic fibre (usually polyester), rather than ordinary sewing thread. I will be sewing leather later in this book, using an 18/5 waxed linen thread. This type of thread is available from handi-craft stores.

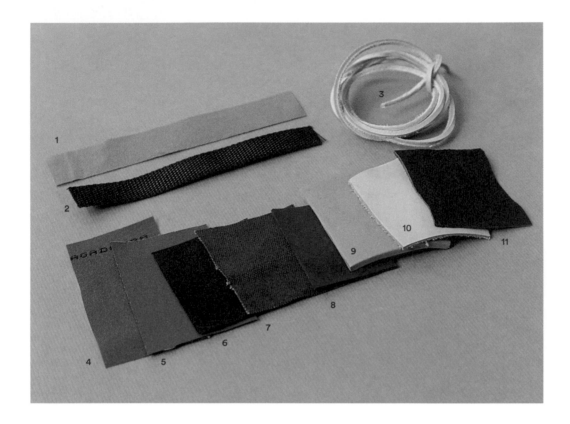

1 Bias binding

2 20 mm polyester webbing

3 Leather strap

4 Cotton/polyester poplin

5 Cotton/polyester canvas

6 Nylon cordura

7 Thick cotton canvas

8 2 mm padding

9 4 mm sleeping pad

10 Natural leather
   (*c.*2 mm thickness)

11 Thinner black leather

BIAS BINDING

To hide the seams on the inside of a bag, preventing the cut edges of the fabric from being visible, you can sew bias binding over the seams. I tend to use a 25–30 mm wide cotton tape. Thinner tapes are simpler to sew; things often get a little thick if you use too sturdy a bias binding. The binding has no function other than to hide a seam and make the bag look neater on the inside. You'll find bias binding in ordinary fabric shops, where it is sometimes also known as bias tape.

STRAPS

Woven straps made from polyester, nylon or cotton can be used as adjustment straps or for other details, e.g. for attaching things to the outside of a backpack. Availability in ordinary fabric shops can sometimes be poor, and you may need to look around to find what you want, particularly if it isn't black webbing straps. 20–25 mm is an adequate width for backpack straps and detailing. Well-stocked fabric shops and hobby craft stores tend to sell black polyester webbing straps.

LEATHER

Leather details are both durable and attractive, and give a nice crafty feel to the product. There are many different qualities of leather available, depending on the type of skin it is made from and which tanning method has been used to produce it. Yes, skin. Though we might not like to think about it, leather is in fact the skin of an animal, preserved as a result of the tanning process, which makes it strong and prevents it from rotting. Simply put: skin becomes leather through tanning. It's a complex process with around 25 distinct steps, and it takes a number of weeks to naturally tan a skin. Cow, ox, goat and sheep leather is common, but exotic skins from lizards and snakes are also available. It's even possible to make leather from fish skin. Tanning is an ancient human skill; there is evidence to suggest that on the border between Pakistan and India, the tanning of skin took place as early as 7000 BC.

There is enough to say about leather to fill an entire book, but generally, it's possible to divide leather into vegetable tanned (natural) and chrome (mineral) tanned. Chrome-tanned leather is most common; the vast majority of all leather production is carried out in this way, with all imaginable qualities and appearances. A soft, supple leather has, in all likelihood, been chrome-tanned. During the chrome tanning process, chromium sulphates are used to preserve the leather, rather than vegetable tannins.

Vegetable, or natural tanning, is a refined version of the original method, where the tannic acid needed to preserve the skin comes from the tannins in bark. Mimosa, chestnut, spruce and oak are all used, and they each give the leather a slightly different feeling and colour. Vegetable tanning is more environmentally friendly than chrome tanning. The leather it produces is also stiffer than chrome-tanned varieties, and has the attractive quality of ageing in a beautiful way. An uncoloured, naturally tanned cow skin is almost white when newly tanned, but once it is exposed to UV radiation from the sun, it will gradually darken and the leather will eventually develop a beautiful cognac brown patina.

Leather is available in many different thicknesses. Goat skin is thinner than cow skin, and the thickest skins, which can be up to 5–6 mm, tend to come from large oxen and water buffalo. This type of leather is often used in saddle production. For the projects in this book, I primarily use leather for straps and detailing. I've used an uncoloured, vegetable tanned cow leather with a thickness of roughly 2–2.5 mm. Any thicker than that, and the leather becomes difficult to sew using an ordinary domestic sewing machine. If the leather needs to be sewn double anywhere, it's best to sew by hand. The material becomes too thick otherwise, meaning that seams sewn using a machine look less attractive.

If you don't want to use animal products, it's perfectly possible to swap the leather for artificial leather (also known as PU, or faux/fake leather). It's considerably cheaper than genuine leather, and works just as well in the majority of cases. It also requires no maintenance. The downsides are primarily the feel, its resistance to tearing, and the fact that the surface of artificial leather tends to crack as it ages. As straps, artificial leather is less suitable; it's best to use polyester here, or to make straps from the same materials you are using on the outside.

ZIPS

Zips, or zippers, are an important component in the majority of heavy-duty projects. The very first zip was patented by Elias Howe, the inventor of the modern sewing machine, in 1851. Howe's precursor to the modern zip never went into production, however, and it was only in 1917 that Swedish-American Gideon Sundbäck and Talon Inc. launched the type of zip we now use. Schott NYC, which continues to

From left: coil zip, vislon zip, metal zip.

23

produce leather jackets to this day, was the first to use zips on items of clothing, in 1925. Zips are often subjected to a large amount of stress, for example when trying to close an overloaded bag. It can be quite a laborious task to replace a broken zip, so no matter which type you choose for your project, you should always aim for high quality. Companies like YKK and Opti both produce a variety of high quality zips. There are a number of types to choose from, so here is a summary of the most common:

➤ COIL ZIPS are absolutely the most common, and also the cheapest. The teeth, made from injection-moulded polyester, resemble a spiral, and they hook onto one another when the zip is closed. Coil zips are available by the metre or in ready-cut lengths. Two key advantages of this type of zip are that they are easy to sew through, therefore hiding the ends, and that they are flexible (the zip doesn't have to be straight to work). This type of zip is often mistakenly called a nylon zip, because they were previously made from nylon.

➤ METAL ZIPS consist of small, individual metal teeth sandwiched together on a polyester tape. This type of zip most resembles Gideon Sundbäck's original from 1917, and is used on items like jeans, bags and coats, often where the zip is a visible detail. The teeth are usually made from aluminium, but other metals like brass and nickel are also used.

➤ VISLON ZIPS resemble the metal zip in their construction, in that they have individual teeth attached to a fabric band. In this case, the teeth are made from plastic rather than metal. The vislon zip is lighter than the metal zip and more weatherproof than the coil zip, which is why they are often used on boat coverings, for example.

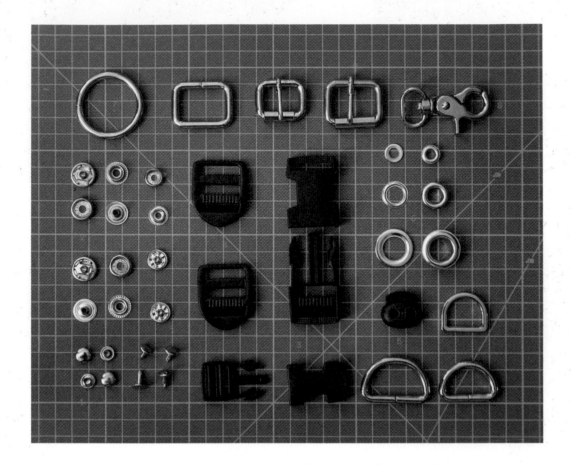

1 Rivets

2 Press-studs

3 Buckle clips

4 Strap adjusters

5 Cord locks

6 Eyelets

7 Various rings

8 Snaphooks

9 Buckles

VARIOUS METAL AND PLASTIC DETAILS

A number of other details are needed to be able to complete a sewing project: press-studs, buckles, rivets and eyelets. To find the right kind of hardware, try a shop selling handicraft materials, or a well-stocked haberdashery. Aim for high quality here, too – it's no fun if a buckle or press-stud breaks because you've been stingy.

EQUIPMENT

SEWING MACHINE

The most important, and most expensive tool you'll need for heavy-duty sewing is a sewing machine. Mahatma Gandhi is said to have called the sewing machine one of mankind's few truly useful inventions, so the investment will likely pay off – you'll get plenty of use out of a sewing machine at home. Just imagine the huge amount of work the sewing machine has saved humankind, given that everything made before its introduction to the market was sewn by hand, stitch by stitch.

The history of the sewing machine begins around 1790, when an Englishman called Thomas Saint invented the very first one – completely from wood! Saint's sewing machine produced a chain stitch, where one thread loops around itself to produce a continuous chain of thread. This technique is still used on many pairs of jeans today, for example on the hem by the ankles. The reason the stitch is still used is primarily cosmetic – because it was used on earlier models – but it is also partly economic. Since chain stitch doesn't involve a bobbin thread that will need to be changed, it's faster to use on an industrial scale. The one great disadvantage is, however, that it can come loose if the thread breaks anywhere in the chain.

The most common sewing machine stitch today is the lock stitch. It's a stitch that uses two threads: an upper thread and a lower thread. The upper thread, the one threaded through the needle, is caught by a rotating hook, which then wraps it around the lower thread. This intertwining of the two threads is hidden inside the material. A lockstitch seam looks the same from both sides of the fabric – straight stitches one after another – while a chain stitch features flat stitches on the top side and looks like a plait beneath.

Overlock is another common stitch used when, for example, sewing t-shirts, underwear and other items of clothing, usually in stretchy material, or to finish off an edge when a folded hem isn't needed. Overlock stitching consists of both straight stitches and a stitch around the edge of the material, to prevent it from unravelling. There is no need for a hem when using an overlock stitch, which is why it is much quicker than ordinary straight stitching. In addition, the machine will cut away any excess material.

In the nineteenth century, sewing machines were being developed in parallel in a number of different areas of the world, but primarily in the

LEFT Industrial machine with a walking foot and free arm.

BELOW Different stitches on one pair of jeans. From top: lock stitch, chain stitch and overlock.

UK and US. In 1832, American Walter Hunt built the first machine to use lock stitch, the technique which virtually all sewing machines today use. During the latter half of the century, the techniques that developed alongside the early machines were used to create cheaper, better machines that were suitable for mass production. A number of patent disputes emerged, with Elias Howe (who also patented the zip) and Isaac Merritt Singer emerging triumphant. Both became multi-millionaires thanks to their sewing machines, and Isaac Merritt founded the Singer Corporation, which, even today, is one of the world's biggest manufacturers of sewing machines.

DOMESTIC AND INDUSTRIAL SEWING MACHINES

An industrial sewing machine is the best type of machine for heavy-duty sewing. They're solidly built to be able to sew quickly, precisely and through thick materials, and to do so for hours at a time. They have powerful external motors that use a belt to drive the sewing machine itself. The sewing machine is fastened to a table, and the motor is beneath the table top; an entire piece of furniture which, unfortunately, most people probably don't have room for at home. In addition, industrial sewing machines are expensive. There are many different types of industrial machine, built for different purposes. The older models aren't quite so expensive, and if you have space for one, they really can't be beaten. But, since the majority of people don't have that kind of space at home, I plan to put those to one side and focus on domestic sewing machines instead. All the projects in this book are made using an ordinary domestic machine. These are sometimes also known as hobby machines.

Domestic sewing machines are portable and, unlike their industrial relatives, have inbuilt motors. Since the machines are compact (built to fit on a table while you're working and to be stashed away in a wardrobe when you're not), there isn't room for such a powerful motor. Even the mechanism transferring the rotation of the motor to the up and down of the needle and the forward and back movement of the feed dogs has to take up less space, and becomes less powerful as a result. This means that domestic sewing machines are unable to handle all thicknesses of material. A few of the projects in this book push the limits of what a domestic machine can really manage, and the result is subsequently less perfect than it would be using an industrial machine. But, in truth, I see that as part of the fun: using what you have to make do.

Unfortunately, the production of sewing machines is no longer what it once was. If you go into a shop and buy a new machine for £300/$400, you'll often walk away with a relatively flimsy plastic machine that doesn't like sewing thick fabrics. This is primarily because the vast majority of the mechanisms (cogs and axles, etc.) inside the machine are made from plastic rather than steel. It's considerably more expensive to produce cogwheels and axles from steel than it is from plastic. Precision and power perform accordingly. On the plus side, you will be taking home quite a bit of computing power; these machines can often sew button holes automatically, and can produce hundreds of patterned stitches that you won't have much need for if you want to sew sturdy objects.

Instead, you should invest in a quality machine from the time when the items produced were durable: the 1950s–70s. The only function you really need is the ability to straight stitch (many industrial machines feature only this option), but you'll often get zigzag stitch for free, and that can be useful to have, even if none of the projects in this book make use of it. Companies known for having produced strong, reliable domestic machines include Husqvarna, Pfaff, Bernina and Singer. Ask a sewing machine repairer (who will often also be selling second-hand, reconditioned machines) what they would recommend for your needs. You should be able to find a very good serviced machine for around £300/$400, or a second hand one from a private seller online for between £150–200/$200–250. The latter can be good, but they may not have been used in a long time, and may need oiling and servicing. Give them a test drive if possible; check that the feed dogs and thread tension work properly and that the machine sews straight. Listen for any odd noises; the machine should be fairly quiet and shouldn't rattle or grate internally. I've made all the projects in this book on a Pfaff 362 from the late 1960s.

If you already have an old machine which should be able to do the job, but which is tangling thread and dropping needles, it probably just needs a service. A repairman will give the machine a once over, oiling it and making adjustments so that the mechanisms work like they should. It costs around £100/$125 to have a sewing machine serviced, which is money well spent.

HOW A SEWING MACHINE WORKS

The needle at the end of the arm moves up and down. It perforates the fabric, and on its way down it passes close to a rotating hook – the loop-taker (or shuttle). At exactly the right moment, the loop-taker passes

a few tenths of a millimetre behind the needle and catches the loop of thread on the back of the needle. (A sewing machine needle has a hollow on one side, pointing backwards in the machine, and it is in this hollow that the loop-taker catches the thread.)

The loop-taker then carries the upper thread, hooking it around the lower thread, which is wound onto a small bobbin around the loop-taker. The two threads have now been intertwined, and when the needle moves upwards it also pulls on the threads, meaning that the seam between the two is pulled into the fabric and hidden. Next, the feed dogs – the toothed surface beneath the presser foot – pull the material forward by one stitch length and the needle moves downwards through the fabric again, repeating its pairing with the loop-taker. So simple and yet so complex.

A domestic machine can sew up to 1,000 stitches a minute, and a fast industrial machine up to 9,000. The sewing machine's various axles, cog wheels and parts work together to ensure that the movement of the needle, the rotation of the loop-taker and the back and forth movement of the feed dogs are precisely synced, enabling them to create a stitch.

The following are other items you will use while sewing:

➤ I. SCISSORS Scissors have a number of uses, like cutting fabric, leather, straps and threads – so buy a good quality pair. I use a pair of household scissors from Fiskars, but much more expensive and attractive tailor's scissors are available.

➤ 2. ROTARY CUTTER Used primarily for cutting leather. A sturdy rotary cutter with removable blades works well. Cheap Stanley knives work less well for cutting leather.

➤ 3. METAL RULER Used alongside the rotary cutter to achieve perfectly straight lines when cutting leather.

➤ 4. PINS Needed for pinning pieces of material into the right position prior to sewing them together. Available with both plastic heads, which are better for thicker materials, and with small metal heads for thinner fabrics.

➤ 5. TAILOR'S CHALK Use this to draw out your pattern on the fabric and decide how to cut out the pieces. Tailor's chalk rubs off, so it won't leave any marks.

➤ 6. MASKING TAPE Sometimes used when you want to apply glue to a specific area but not outside it. Buy a good brand, i.e. 3M – you'll find out why if you don't follow this advice.

➤ 7. CONTACT ADHESIVE Used to stick together pieces of material that are difficult to pin or which need to sit very precisely before they're sewn together. It's applied with a brush that will eventually turn into a solid lump, but you'll be able to apply the glue anyway. Water-based contact adhesive is available, and it works just as well as its smellier predecessor.

➤ 8. TRACING WHEEL When making clothing, tracing wheels are used alongside carbon paper to, for example, transfer a pattern onto fabric. I rarely use tracing wheels for this given that the patterns in heavy-duty sewing are often fairly simple, and a chalk and ruler are usually a better choice. I do, however, use a tracing wheel to mark where I am going to punch holes in my leather when hand sewing. Using a pronged diamond chisel is also possible here, but I tend to use a tracing wheel for simpler leather projects.

➤ 9. AWL Used to punch holes in leather when hand sewing.

➤ 10. LEATHER EDGE BEVELLER Used to round corners on leather straps or other details. Doing so isn't strictly necessary — you can keep the corners straight — but rounded leather corners do look good.

11. LEATHER NEEDLES Thicker and with a slightly larger eye than ordinary sewing needles. They are also slightly less sharp, since the stitch holes are punched in advance (using an awl) when hand-sewing leather. A slightly shorter darning needle with its tip blunted will work just as well.

12. RIVET SETTER Used to set rivets. I bought mine in India.

13. PRESS-STUD SETTER Used to attach press-studs. Use a cutting board or steady piece of wood as an underlay.

14. EYELET TOOL A simple eyelet tool will often be included with any eyelets you buy. If you're going to be attaching a lot of eyelets, it is a good idea to use a metal tool similar to the one used for rivets.

15. HAMMER Used to hit rivets and eyelets and to hammer glued joins. An ordinary hammer will work perfectly well here, as will a smaller one with a ball on the reverse (as overleaf).

16. SEWING MACHINE OIL A must to keep your machine running smoothly.

17. SEWING MACHINE NEEDLES Use 90/14 jeans needles or 100/16 fabric needles, and 90/14 leather needles for leather detailing.

18. HEADTORCH Perfect for achieving good lighting when you're working on small details and need to be able to see particularly well.

19. THIMBLE Good to have when sewing by hand, and can be made of leather as below.

20. SEAM RIPPER Used to unpick seams.

21. TWEEZERS Used to remove threads once seams have been unpicked.

22. LIGHTER Used to burn the ends of straps or threads, etc.

23. SEWING THREAD

24. WAXED THREAD For sewing leather.

25. HOLE PUNCH For punching holes in leather. As ever, you tend to get what you pay for. Avoid the cheapest models; they won't last.

26. PRECISION SCREWDRIVERS For adjusting the sewing machine, i.e. the tension of the lower thread.

27. MEASURING TAPE Used constantly. Buy a spare, because they're cheap and tend to disappear.

Not pictured: PLASTIC CUTTING MAT WITH GRID Works well as an underlay when cutting leather; the grid pattern simplifies the orientation when cutting.

Not pictured: IRON For pressing seams. In truth, a steam iron is best, but an old iron without steam function will also work well enough.

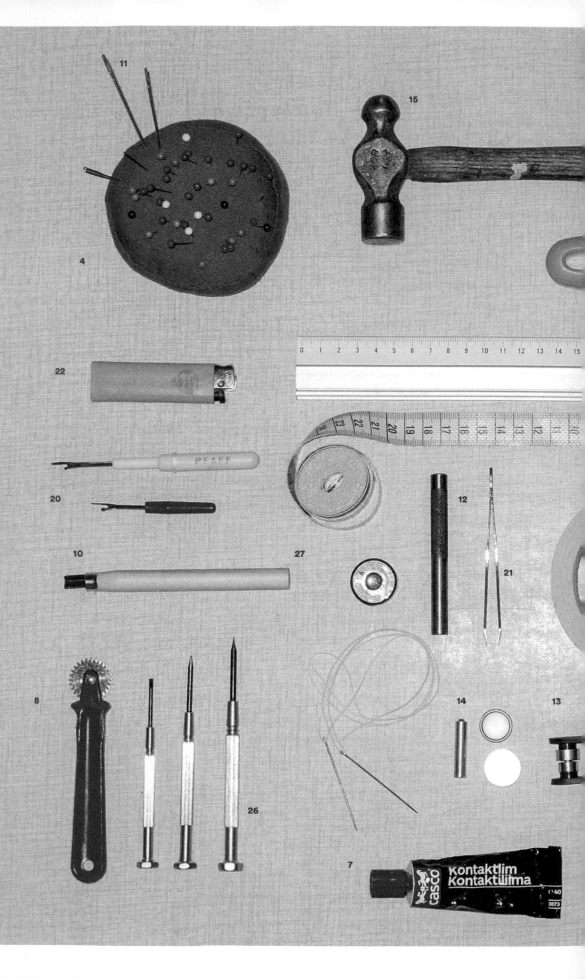

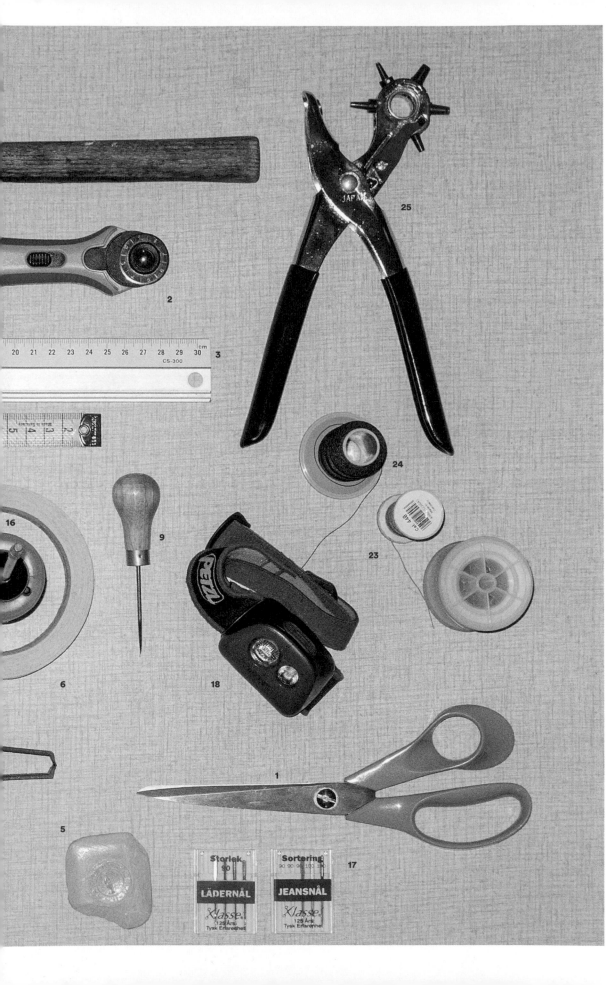

WORKING METHODS AND TIPS

SEWING ON A MACHINE

Are you someone who never took your sewing machine proficiency test in home economics? The good thing about using a sewing machine is that you can never be pulled over for doing it wrong. Anyone can learn how to sew; it's just a case of stepping on the gas. Here are a few basic pointers you may find useful.

THREADING THE MACHINE

Upper thread

In order for your needlework to look neat and attractive, the upper thread needs to be properly threaded. The upper thread's spool sits on a pin on top of the machine, and the thread should pass through several small eyelets and around a tension disk, followed by several more eyelets, before being threaded through the needle itself – from the front, going backwards. If you're unsure how your particular machine should be threaded, there are instruction manuals for the majority of older models online. Follow the instructions for how to thread your machine to the letter, because the idea is that the thread should be at the exact right tension when you sew. Cut the end of the thread with a sharp pair of scissors and make sure you have a clean cut that isn't fraying – this will make it easier to thread through the eye of the needle. Flatten the end of the thread by pressing it (the eye of the needle is oval, rather than round). Hold the thread roughly 1 cm from the end, take aim and thread through the hole.

Lower thread

The lower thread is needed to produce a stitch; the two threads intertwine and, if the thread tension is set correctly, the join between them should be hidden inside the material. Before you can begin sewing, this means you need to wind the lower thread onto the bobbin. Every now and again, when you eventually start sewing – and often during a critical moment – the lower thread will run out, and you'll have to stop work to wind on more thread.

Check the instruction manual for your sewing machine to find out how to wind the bobbin. The general idea is that you wind some of the upper

Threading the lower thread.

thread through a guide and around a tension disk, after which you wind the end onto the bobbin, which is placed on a small pin. A pedal or button will set the pin in motion, winding thread onto the bobbin.

Next, you place the bobbin in its capsule and pull out around 20 cm of thread. Check your instruction manual to make sure the thread is running the right way in the capsule, this is important for ensuring that the thread tension is correct. The bobbin is then slotted into the rotating shuttle behind the cover at the very end of the sewing machine arm. The capsule fits precisely into the shuttle, and will click into place. All that's left to do now is to fish out the lower thread by turning the hand wheel (see image on p. 30) towards you – i.e. anti-clockwise – so that the machine moves 'forward'. The needle, threaded with the upper thread, will pass through the gap in the feed dogs, meet the shuttle and fish out the end of the lower thread. Pull both threads backwards, beneath the presser foot.

THREAD TENSION

Setting the tension of the upper thread

Correct thread tension is crucial to achieving neat, durable stitches. The upper and lower threads should meet in the middle of the fabric, preferably as close to the mid-point in terms of depth as possible. The thread tension assembly (see image on p. 31) through which you threaded the upper thread between the tension disks behind it, often comes with a scale of 1–10, where 1 is loosest and 10 tightest. Set the thread tension to somewhere in the middle of the scale, around 5 or 6, and test the tension by sewing together two pieces of fabric that are the same thickness as the material you want to use. Check the seam. If the lower thread is being pulled up through the fabric so that the interweaving of the two threads is visible between stitches on the right side of the material, the upper thread tension is too tight. If, instead, the upper thread is being pulled down so far that it is visible on the underside of the fabric, and if the under thread is almost straight along the stitch, the upper thread tension is too loose. Adjust the thread tension and keep testing until you are happy with the result. Note that the thread tension is not activated when the presser foot is folded up – in other words, it's only once the presser foot has been folded down that you can check the thread tension currently set on the dial. If the presser foot is folded up, the upper thread will not be taut (in order to enable you to pull through more loose thread).

Adjusting the lower thread tension

The tension of the lower thread can also be adjusted, though it is fairly uncommon to need to do so. If you are unable to produce a neat stitch by adjusting the tension of the upper thread, this may mean that the tension of the lower thread has not been properly set up. It can be adjusted using the screw on the bobbin case. If you tighten the screw slightly, you will increase the tension of the lower thread. You may need to do this when using a very thin or very thick thread. If your lower thread tends to be visible on the top of the material, despite having a low upper thread tension, you probably need to increase the lower thread tension. The same principle applies in the opposite case: if the upper thread is still visible on the underside of the material, despite a high upper thread tension, the lower thread tension needs to be lowered.

Thread tension for different material thicknesses

A thick fabric, or several layers of fabric, will behave very differently in the sewing machine to a thin fabric, which means that the machine needs to be adjusted to the specific material you are working with. Always test sew using the correct fabric when you are checking and adjusting the thread tension. As a general rule of thumb, a thicker fabric will need a higher thread tension than a thin one. With a bit of practice, you'll get a feel for thread tension, and you'll learn to adjust it without doing trial runs – for example when you move from sewing two layers of material to four, i.e. thicker overall, meaning the upper thread tension needs to be increased slightly.

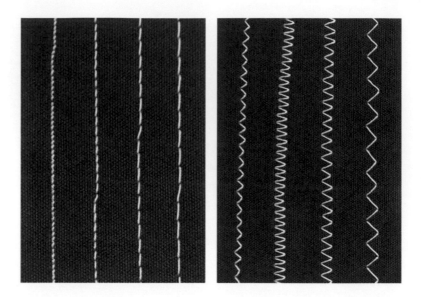

Straight and zigzag
stitches with different
stitch lengths and widths.

STITCH LENGTH AND FEED DOGS

A straight stitch can have different stitch lengths – different distances between the holes where the thread passes through the material, in other words.

For more robust sewing, it's a good idea for your stitch length not to be too short; 3–4 mm tends to be enough. Your sewing machine will have a stitch length dial, which will likely be marked with a scale of 1–4. It is the movement of the feed dogs that regulates the stitch length. The longer the stitch, the more the feed dogs need to pull the material forward as the needle makes its way up and down. If the feed dogs do not move at all, the machine will sew stitch after stitch into the same point on the material. The feed dogs are the toothed strips beneath the presser foot. They clamp the material against the presser foot, and as the feed dogs make their down-forward-up-back movement, the teeth press it against the presser foot and draw it forward.

A zigzag stitch is, in principal, the same as a straight stitch, with the difference that the needle also moves sideways, piercing the material to the left and the right, respectively – hence why the stitches form a zigzag pattern. Using the stitch width dial (see image on p. 30), you can adjust the width of the zigzag stitches. A wide stitch with a short stitch length is good if you want to sew an edge. To return to a straight stitch, you just need to set the stitch width dial back to 0.

The machine is now ready for the sewing you have planned, and it's time to get to work.

Sewing a straight stitch

Place the pieces of fabric you want to sew together beneath the presser foot, at the point where you want to begin sewing. This should ideally be along one edge, to form a seam. Fold down the presser foot and turn the hand wheel to manually drive the machine forward, checking that everything is working properly – help it get going, in other words – and then gently press on the pedal so that the motor takes over and the machine starts to sew. Secure the thread by sewing a few forward stitches and a few backstitches. You do this by pressing down the backstitch control, then continuing with your forward stitching. Sew along the length you had planned, and finish off by securing the seam with more forward and backstitches.

When taking the material out of the machine, turn the hand wheel so that the needle is in its highest position. This will release the upper thread from the shuttle and allow it to be easily pulled out. If the tip of the needle is close to the surface of the fabric, the threads will be locked in place by the shuttle, and you won't be able to pull out the thread when you try to remove the fabric. Cut the threads by the final stitch and allow roughly 20 cm of upper and lower thread to stick out of the machine. Pull these threads back, beneath the presser foot, and the machine is ready to be used again.

Changing a sewing machine needle

Sewing machine needles do occasionally break, often as a result of sewing too quickly on several layers of thick fabric. To change the needle, loosen the wing nut to the right of the needle attachment. The needle has a front and back, and should be inserted with the flat edge pointing backwards and the round edge towards you.

Sewing techniques

A couple of common sewing techniques that will be useful in heavy-duty sewing are plain seams, topstitch and hemming.

To sew a plain seam, you place two pieces of fabric on top of one another, edge to edge, then straight stitch along their length, roughly

10–15 mm from the edge. When you then turn out the joined pieces of fabric, the needlework will be entirely hidden on the inside. This is the most common stitch used in the projects in this book. If you're using a fabric with a right and a wrong side, the materials should be placed face to face when you join them with a seam.

Topstitch simply refers to sewing one piece of fabric onto another – adding an exterior pocket, for example. Typically, the edges of the fabric being added on top will be folded in and pressed with an iron. Afterwards, you simply sew the top piece of fabric onto the one below using a row of stitches several millimetres from the edge.

A hem is the end of a piece of material where the edge of a piece of fabric has been folded twice and pressed, forming a flat tunnel of material. A hem can be narrow or wide, depending on your preferences or requirements. First, fold and press let's say 1 cm of fabric, then fold a second time and press. Your hem is ready to sew.

French seams are another technique which can be used to enclose the cut edges of material, hiding them from view and making any zigzag or overlocking stitches unnecessary. This is, however, less suitable on thick materials, as it becomes fairly clumsy; it works best on thinner fabrics.

SEWING MACHINE TIPS AND TRICKS

We've now learnt to set up the machine and to sew a simple straight stitch and zigzag stitch. With a bit of practice, that's all you'll need to be able to complete the projects in this book, and also to create your own projects in future. With that said, there are a few other considerations which will improve your results. Here are some tips.

Plan your needlework

Think through what you want the machine to do before you start sewing. Think about starting at the right end, about how you will turn and move your work in the machine when you need to change direction, and where and how your stitches will end. The most common mistake in machine sewing is to sew first and think later. Doing so often ends in unpicking.

Sew truly straight stitches

To achieve a good end product, it's important that your stitches are straight and don't trail off to the sides. Using your tailor's chalk, draw the line you want the stitches to follow on the material, then follow it. It's difficult to produce straight, neat stitches without something for the eye to follow.

Turning the material

When you're sewing a row of stitches that need to turn by 90 degrees (or any other angle), stop sewing at the point where the change in direction will take place. Keep the needle down, raise the presser foot and rotate the piece of material by the desired angle. Continue sewing in the new direction.

Upper thread stitches outwards, if possible

The stitches formed by the upper thread tend to look a little better than those produced by the lower thread, even if a perfectly set-up machine is supposed to produce equally attractive stitches on the top and bottom. A good tip when sewing visible seams is to try to sew with the outside of the material upwards in the machine. If you do this, it will be the upper thread that is ultimately visible. Sadly, this isn't always possible. When sewing a pocket to the inside of a bag, for example, or in many other instances, you'll have to sew with the inside upwards in order to make sure you are placing the stitches perfectly along the edge of the pocket. The stitches that will be visible in this instance are those formed by the lower thread, which is why it is especially important that the thread tension is correct, so that the stitches are equally neat on both sides.

Seam allowance

When joining two pieces of material with a seam, the excess material is known as the seam allowance. Make sure your seam allowance isn't too small – this can result in the fabric tearing and the seam breaking. Between 10 and 15 mm tends to be enough, but ideally never less than 10 mm. If your seam allowance is too large, you can always give it a trim by cutting away any excess. Just make sure to keep at least 10 mm.

Adding bias binding

When you want to use bias binding to cover a seam with a 10–15 mm seam allowance – on the inside of a bag, for example – 25–30 mm wide binding is suitable. Begin by folding the binding in half lengthwise. Next, you can move the binding into position over the seam, and slowly sew through both the binding and seam – there's no need to pin, in other words. As a general rule, pinning is useful in the beginning, before you're used to the processes, but the more confident you become, the less you will find yourself pinning things.

Sewing thick materials

The biggest problem with domestic sewing machines is that their motors and mechanisms are too feeble to be able to sew very thick materials. The needle simply won't be able to force its way through the material, the gap beneath the presser foot will be too small, and the movement of the feed dogs beneath the fabric will not be enough to achieve an attractive finished product. However, if you pay attention to when the machine starts to struggle and immediately help it out by using the hand wheel, powering the motor gently with your foot, it is still possible to sew very thick materials – albeit slowly. A good domestic machine should be able to handle up to six layers of thick canvas, but that's if you are essentially driving the machine by hand and have the presser foot at its highest position – you can help pull the material forward slightly. Use a long stitch length and be patient.

LEATHERWORK

Leather detailing is attractive and hard-wearing, and, if you use a vegetable-tanned leather, it will also age beautifully. For the projects in this book, you won't need any advanced leatherwork techniques. All you will need to be able to do is to cut out your pieces, often in the form of straps, from a larger piece of leather, occasionally hand sewing them together to make handles and then sewing them firmly into place.

Using a rotary cutter, you can cut leather straps and details with precise, straight edges; something that is more difficult with an ordinary utility or Stanley knife. Place a metal ruler along the line you want to cut, and press the rotary cutter firmly against the leather on the cutting mat while gently following the line of the ruler. If you push forward at a slow, steady pace, you'll end up with the perfect cut.

Once you've cut out the leather – to use as a handle, for example – it looks good if you round off the corners. I use a chisel for this. You can buy

Hand sewn leather handles in the firewood holder project (see p. 72).

special edging tools for leather, but they aren't too easy to get hold of, so I tend to use one designed for sculpting wood. Place the chisel at the edge you want to round off, line it up carefully and give it a firm (but not hard) tap with the hammer.

Hand sewing

Hand sewing leather is extremely easy, very hard-wearing, and it looks good. Plus, it's a fairly relaxed and contemplative process.

Draw out the line you want to sew along. It's common to place the stitches roughly 3–4 mm from the edge, depending on the thickness of the leather. Use an awl to mark out exactly where you want the line to start and end, and, using the tip, carefully scratch a line into the leather between the two points. Next, roll the tracing wheel along this line to

45

mark where you will pierce holes with the awl. There are roughly 2.5 mm between the points on my tracing wheel, so I pierce a hole in every other one and, as a result, end up with 5 mm between stitches. Don't make your stitches too short, that won't look good on leather. Somewhere between 4–6 mm will be fine. Use the awl to pierce a hole in the leather at each needle point.

Take two leather needles and a length of waxed thread, and thread a needle onto each end of the thread. To sew something like a handle, the leather will be folded in half lengthways. Place the holes that will be sewn together on top of one another, and pull the needle and thread through both holes. Reinforce the first stitch by sewing one or two stitches around the edge with each needle and then pulling on the thread. Continue by pushing both needles through the next hole, the second one in the opposite direction to the first, and pull again. Continue until you have stitched each hole, and make sure you pull on each stitch equally hard. Finish off your seam and secure the thread by stitching around the edge with each needle and then pushing the needle through the eyelet in both cases. Finally, pull the thread and cut close to the knot.

Sewing leather details with a machine

Attaching leather handles or other details to fabric works well with a sewing machine. Use the awl to mark out thin lines where you want your stitches to go. To stop the leather from moving before you sew it to the fabric, it may be a good idea to glue it into place. Tape around the area of fabric to be glued so that none will seep out and be visible. Apply a thin layer of glue to both surfaces and allow to dry until the glue is no longer tacky – roughly 2–3 minutes – before pressing the two together. Change to a leather needle before you begin sewing. Bring the needle down at the exact point where your line starts, and drive the machine by hand using the hand wheel, with your foot lightly pressing the pedal to help it forward. Sew one stitch at a time, and take care to make sure they are all the same length and follow the line exactly. When you reach a corner, turn the same way you would with any other material. Finish off by stitching back and forth on the same hole a few times. As when sewing several layers of thick material, it's patience and care which produce good results here.

I have used natural vegetable-tanned leather for the details and handles in my projects. This type of leather gives the products a natural look, and will develop a beautiful patina over time. It also requires slightly more care than a heavily dyed, chrome-tanned leather. Still, it's very easy to take proper care of your leather products.

Clean the leather

The most important step is to clean the leather when it gets dirty. If it's just a bit dusty, a quick wipe after each use with a soft, slightly damp cloth will be enough. If the leather is very dirty, and the dirt also contains fat, you can clean it by first rubbing the damp cloth over a soap – ideally a so-called gall soap, which is made of entirely natural products. Don't use too much soap, start gently and make sure it isn't too wet, and wipe away the dirt with the cloth. Lastly, wipe with a slightly damp cloth free from soap until there is no residue left. Mild hand soap can also work well – soap designed for babies, for example.

Allow the leather to dry

After cleaning, you should leave the leather to dry at room temperature. Drying leather in a tumble drier, drying cupboard, on a radiator or using a hairdryer should be avoided, as doing so will dry out the leather too deeply, making it shrink and possibly even crack. Direct sunlight is bad for leather for the same reason, and prolonged exposure to sunlight can eventually lead to cracks. That doesn't mean you should avoid using your leather products in the sun, however, it just means you shouldn't hang leather out to dry in the sun or in extremely sunny environments – i.e. on sailing boats.

Conditioning your leather

Once the leather is clean and dry, it's time to condition it. This doesn't need to be done every time you clean your leather, 2–3 times a year is usually enough – often after a more thorough clean. This can be done with leather grease, leather oil or leather balsam. A little Vaseline or military balm will also work well. For smaller leather details, as in the projects in this book, leather grease is easiest. Leather grease contains a mix of wax and various fats; the harder it is, the more wax it contains. The wax acts like a protective layer on top of the leather, and the fat penetrates beneath the surface. Try to use natural products made from beeswax and vegetable fats where possible.

Take a small amount of leather grease onto a cotton cloth and rub it evenly over the leather. Work the grease into the leather and then wipe away any excess. If the leather still feels dry, repeat the process. The most common mistake is to apply too much grease too often. This can eventually lead to the pores of the leather becoming filled, weakening the fibres of the material. The grease will also give the leather a deeper tone. Test how much to use on a less visible area of the leather before you apply to the remainder.

Leather oil is typically used on larger leather products such as sofas, since it's simpler and quicker to apply to a large surface. Leather balsam is essentially oil or fat mixed with some kind of solvent, which helps the oils to sink into the leather. Balsam doesn't tend to make the leather much darker, and it's harder to overuse.

It's difficult to give precise advice around the use of grease, oil and balsam, and there are varying opinions on the subject. The most important point is that you clean your leather when it gets dirty and then condition it several times a year.

TEXTILE CARE

Taking care of the other fabrics in your projects is primarily a case of wiping them with a damp cloth and possibly using a little soap, if necessary. If a bag gets particularly dirty, I tend to put it through a 40 degree wash in the machine, but it's probably better to hand wash. Leather details don't really benefit from being machine washed, and metal rivets can sometimes leave permanent black marks on leather, but I like to think of that as being part of the patina process. Leather is usually fine if you leave it to dry slowly, stretch it carefully and condition it afterwards.

Waxing fabric

If your fabric is cotton or a cotton/polyester mix, you can also wax it. Textile wax is often a mixture of beeswax and paraffin. You gently warm the lump of wax (holding it in your hand is often enough) and then rub it against the material. Next, you set the wax into the fabric using an iron, hairdryer or – very carefully – heat gun. You'll often need to repeat the process several times for the material to be thoroughly waxed. The waxing process gives a certain level of water resistance, but once the material is wet (after a heavy rain shower, for example), it will dry more slowly than un-waxed fabric. As a result, it's really a matter of taste as to whether you should wax your fabrics or not. I prefer to use a very dense un-waxed fabric that will keep the water out instead. Wax gives a slightly stiff, robust feeling to material. Synthetic fabrics aren't suitable for waxing, as they don't tolerate heat as well as cotton.

PROJECTS

BACKPACK

TIME: 20 HOURS | LEVEL 4

This backpack, at around 26 litres, is a good size for day trips in the countryside; it's perfect for carrying a portable stove or coffee pot, some spare warm clothes, food, a thermos, water, and maybe even a little wood and equipment. It's also big enough for a 2–3 night stay when travelling. The backpack has two large pockets on the front, a padded back and bottom, and straps on the side for attaching a fishing rod or other equipment.

MATERIAL

– densely woven polyester/ cotton canvas for outer, *c.*100 × 150 cm
– cotton/polyester poplin lining, *c.*100 × 150 cm
– cordura nylon for bottom, 33 × 25 cm (or use same material as outer)
– sleeping mat for padding, 4 mm thickness, 30 × 22 + 33 × 55 cm
– thin foam, 1–2 mm thickness, 20 mm wide, *c.*125 cm length
– strap adjusters, 20 mm (× 2)
– rivets, 10 mm (× 10)
– coil zip with 2 sliders, size 5, 50 cm
– polyester webbing, 20 mm width, 4 metres
– plastic clips, 20 mm (× 4)
– bias binding, 30 mm width, *c.*5 metres
– eyelets, 10 mm (× 12)
– leather cord, 125 cm
– buckle, 20 mm width
– leather strap, 630 × 20 mm

MATERIAL FOR BODY OF BACKPACK

This backpack is shaped like a cylinder, and the bottom piece is rectangular with rounded corners. A leather cord threaded through eyelets at the top of the bag can be used to close the backpack. The top of the cylinder is missing, replaced by a lid that is sewn on at the back.

Use Fig. 1 to make a paper pattern for the bottom piece, then trace around this on the outer material and the lining. Add a seam allowance of 15 mm at each side.

Cut out the lining and outer. I had a piece of cordura left over from another project, and since it is water resistant, I decided to use that as my bottom piece. You can just use the same material as elsewhere on the bag.

Use the paper pattern (without the seam allowance) to draw the same shape onto a piece of padding. Cut out the padding and then cut away roughly 3 mm from each edge, so that the piece is slightly smaller than the bottom itself.

Apply a thin layer of contact adhesive to the piece of padding and the bottom section. Allow the glue to dry for several minutes, until it no longer feels tacky, and then press the pieces together. As the padding is slightly smaller than the bottom section, there should be an even gap of *c.*18 mm around each side.

30 cm

21.5 cm

Radius = 10 cm

Fig. 1 Pattern for
bottom piece.

Glue the lining to the padding in the same way, using a thin layer of glue. The material hanging over the edges of the padding does not need to be glued. If you prefer, you can skip this gluing stage completely, but using glue gives a slightly sturdier bottom section.

The fabric for the main body of the bag should measure 72 × 55 cm (incl. seam allowance), and the back piece should be 33 × 55 cm (incl. seam allowance). Draw these pieces onto the outer material and cut out.

Next, draw and cut out a piece of padding for the back (29 × 35 cm) as well as a piece of lining for the back (33 × 47 cm).

POCKET ON INSIDE OF BACK SECTION

Draw and cut out a 24 × 28 cm piece of lining. This will be the pocket on the inside of the back section.

If you want your backpack to have a laptop pocket, make this pocket large enough to hold your laptop and then position it a few centimetres above the bottom edge.

Fold, press and sew a 2 cm hem at the top edge of the pocket, then fold and press roughly 12 mm along the sides and bottom of the pocket.

Pin the pocket onto the piece of lining that will be sewn into the back of the bag. Mark out the middle of the pocket and the lining to make it easier to put into position. I place my pocket vertically in roughly the middle of the back piece.

Sew the pocket onto the lining. Start and finish by securing the thread.

PREPARE THE BACK SECTION

The back section of your backpack consists of outer material, sleeping mat and lining (with pocket), and this needs to be glued and sewn together. First, cut out an extra piece of outer material, 33 × 22 cm, and glue it to the inside of the outer, up against the top edge. This is a reinforcement and will make the backpack sturdier at the top, where there is no padding.

Glue the padding to the inside of the outer material, roughly 2 cm from the bottom edge. Applying a few horizontal and vertical lines of glue will be enough (you don't need to cover the entire surface with glue, in other words) to hold the pieces in position – they're all going to be sewn together later anyway. The padding should overlap the piece of outer material you added as reinforcement by roughly 4 cm.

Draw a large cross on the padding, from corner to corner, and then sew these pieces together along these lines. Test sew a piece of padding to a piece of outer material first, to make sure you have the right thread tension. You'll be sewing with the outer fabric facing down (the sewing machine won't function too well with the padding against the feed dogs), and since the lower thread is what will be visible on the outside of the bag, you need to make sure you are producing neat stitches.

Glue the piece of lining with the pocket onto the padding. The pocket should obviously be facing out, and the pieces should line up at the bottom edge. Use a thin layer of glue.

SHOULDER STRAPS

The shoulder straps consist of two identical pieces of outer material whose seam allowance has been folded inwards, each with a thin piece of foam inside. They are sewn together using topstitches around the edges.

Make a true-to-size paper pattern of the shoulder straps, as per Fig. 2. Each should be 5.5 cm wide at the top, 4.5 cm wide at the bottom, and 50 cm long.

Trace four identical shapes onto the outer material, each with a 15 mm seam allowance, and cut out.

Cut out two pieces of thin foam (1–2 mm thickness) to the same measurements, then cut away 3 mm from each edge. Next, cut 3 cm from the top of the foam (it isn't needed in the section where the straps will be attached to the backpack itself, and means fewer layers to sew through).

Glue the foam to the outer material so that you have a 15 mm seam allowance at each edge, then fold the seam allowance over the edges of the foam and glue it down. At the corners and curves, you will need to clip away small wedge shapes from the material to enable your folds to follow the bends nicely.

Press in the seam allowance on the 'upper' pieces of the shoulder straps, clipping and gluing where necessary on the curves to prevent the folds from becoming too thick; you want no more than two layers all the way around. At the lower end, it's easiest to use 45 degree angles rather than small radii. Apply only a very thin layer of glue here; the glue is just to help keep the material in place while you sew. Glue tends to stick to the needle when you sew, even if it has been drying for several hours, and this can lead to ugly stitches, so use as little glue as possible.

Place the 'upper' section on top of the glued lower piece, and sew the two halves of the strap together. As you sew the seam to attach the upper to the

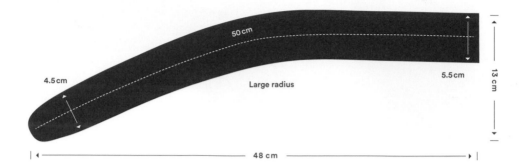

50 cm

4.5 cm

5.5 cm

13 cm

Large radius

48 cm

Fig. 2 Pattern for
shoulder strap
(excluding seam allowance)

lower half (incl. padding), you'll be sewing through four layers of material and padding, so take it very slowly and use the hand wheel to help the machine out all the way around.

Cut out two pieces of leather measuring 20 × 180 mm. Fold them in the middle and mark out holes 1.5 and 7.5 cm, respectively, from the edge where the ends meet (see Fig. 4).

Punch two holes through the folded pieces of leather, a total of four holes in each strap.

Mark out the holes on the shoulder straps, making sure the fold in the leather is lined up with the end of the shoulder strap, and punch the holes using the hole punch.

Cut out four leather circles with a diameter of 18 mm, and punch a hole in the middle of each.

Thread a strap adjuster onto one of the leather straps, fold the leather in half and rivet it into place on the end of the shoulder strap (see Fig. 4). Use 10 mm rivets here, since they have to pass through a number of layers. Do the same with the other shoulder strap, only in mirror image. Your shoulder straps are now ready to be sewn onto the back piece.

THE POCKETS ON THE OUTSIDE OF THE BACKPACK

Cut out two pieces of fabric measuring 27 × 33 cm.

Cut a 24 cm length of zip, thread the slider onto it, and close the zip almost to the end.

Cut a 20 cm hole for the zip 9 cm from the upper edge of the material (along the 27 cm edge).

Press the material so that you are left with a c. 18 mm opening in the

56

shape of a rectangle. Place the zip beneath it, centred in the hole so that there is an equal amount of overlap at each end. Pin and sew into place, with your seams roughly 2–3 mm from the edges (see image below). Now, turn the pocket so that the zip is facing downwards, and pinch in the corners by 45 degrees; your aim here is to make the pocket three-dimensional. Mark where the flaps created by the folds need to be sewn.

Turn the pocket inside out, pin and then sew a 6 cm seam across the flap at each corner; the pocket will be roughly 5 cm deep, with a 1 cm seam allowance.

Cut away any excess material from the folded corners, and press a *c.* 1 cm seam allowance around each corner of the pocket.

Take the piece of material you cut out for the main body and pin the pockets into position. It's important that the pockets are perfectly straight and at the right distance from the centre line. Mark the middle of the material and place the pockets roughly 4 cm apart – i.e. 2 cm to the right and 2 cm to the left of the centre line, roughly 5 cm from the bottom edge.

Cut out four 6 cm lengths of polyester webbing and burn the ends. Thread them on to the female half of a plastic clip and pin the end of the strap beneath the pocket – it will be sewn into place by the seam around the pocket (see Fig. 5).

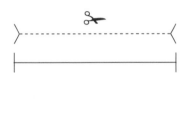

Place a strap + clip at the top and bottom of the outer side of one pocket, 2.5 cm from the upper and lower edges, respectively. Check that the pocket is perfectly straight and that the edges are even – so that there won't be any creases.

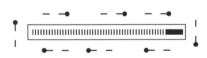

Slowly and carefully, sew around the pocket using top-stitch, adjusting the position as necessary. This is one of the most difficult stages in the project, so take your time. Repeat the same procedure with the second pocket.

CARRY HANDLE

Cut out a 28 × 6 cm piece of outer material, fold it lengthwise down the middle and press.

Fold in the cut edges and press. You should now be left with a *c.* 15 mm wide strap which is four layers of material thick.

Sew along each side, roughly 3 mm from the edge.

SEW TOGETHER THE BACK PIECE
AND SHOULDER STRAPS

Cut a 33 × 8 cm piece of outer material. Fold in and press along the long sides so that the piece of material is now *c.*5 cm wide.

Pin the piece of material to the outer side of the back piece, just above where the padding ends, with the shoulder straps inserted from above, underlapping the piece of material by *c.*3 cm. The distance between the shoulder straps should be *c.*6 cm, and they should be angled a few degrees to follow the curve of the shoulders. Pin and try out a few different configurations to see what suits you best.

Pin the carry handle at the length you want it between the straps, and sew the pieces together along the edge of the material, both at the top and bottom. Next, sew an extra seam 8 mm beneath the upper line. These seams are the most difficult in the entire project, as there are a total of 9 layers of material to sew through.

SEW TOGETHER THE MAIN BODY AND THE BOTTOM

Pin together the bottom and the main body of the bag with the wrong side facing outwards. Do this by marking where the centre points of the front and bottom pieces are, then lining them up.

Sew the two pieces together. Cut away any excess material, leaving a 1 cm seam allowance, and then hide this using bias binding.

Press the bias binding down the middle, lengthwise, before you attach it. The more conscientious among you will clip the binding and glue it first, so that it sits neatly on top of the seam allowance, therefore avoiding any possible creases.

Fig. 4 Details of shoulder strap, strap fastenings and strap end piece.

SHOULDER STRAP TRIANGLES

Cut out two triangles from the outer material, each with a base of 24 cm and a height of 12 cm.

Fold the triangles down the middle, fold in a *c.*1 cm seam allowance on both the top and bottom, and press.

Place a 50 cm length of webbing strap inside each triangle so that its end meets the point of the triangle, and sew together with a seam along the outer edge of the triangle (the eagle-eyed among you will have spotted this in Fig. 4).

Sew around the edges and add an extra row of stitches along the inner edge of the strap as reinforcement.

Fig. 5 The adjustment
strap is sewn into place
in the pocket seam.

Turn the main body and bottom inside out, and pin together with the back piece so that the outside is facing inwards.

Pin the triangles you just made into position in the bottom corners, roughly 1–2 cm above the bottom seam.

Cut four 35 cm lengths of polyester webbing, burn the ends, double fold 1 cm at one end of each, and sew straight across this fold.

Thread the male part of a plastic clip onto each of the four straps and double check that it is the right way up. Next, pin the straps into what will be the side seam. Make sure that they are at the right height and the right way up in relation to the other part of the plastic clips – which you have already sewn into place by the pockets.

Sew the two side seams. Be particularly careful while sewing over the triangles, as the material will be very thick here. Double sew the seams over the triangles before you secure the threads.

Cut away any unnecessary material, leaving roughly 1 cm of seam allowance, then burn the ends of the trimmed straps again. To finish off, sew bias binding onto all of the inside seams.

Next, trim the upper edge of the backpack so that you have a neat line. Fold over roughly 1 cm of material and press. Fold the seam allowance from the side seams out of the way before you begin sewing to avoid having to sew through an unnecessary number of layers. Now, fold the top edge by another 3–4 cm so that the hem lines up exactly with the edge of the lining on the inside of the back piece. Sew the hem roughly 3 mm from the lower edge of the fold. Your finished upper edge should be 7–8 cm away from the point where the shoulder straps are affixed.

The next step is to pierce a number of 10 mm holes for the eyelets, roughly 15 mm from the top edge. The circumference of my bag is 96 cm, and with a distance of 8 cm between each eyelet, that meant 12 in total. Place the two front eyelets an equal distance away from the centre line and then mark out your next holes 8 cm away from that point. Use a hole punch to pierce the holes you have marked, and hammer eyelets into each. Next, lace a 125 cm leather cord through the eyelets and knot each end.

ATTACH THE LID

Fig. 6 shows the pattern for the lid, with dimensions. Make a full-sized paper pattern of the lid, trace it onto the outer material and then cut it out.

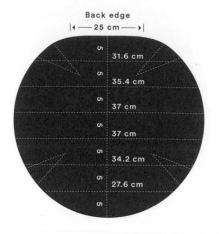

Back edge

|◄ —— 25 cm —— ►|

5   31.6 cm

5   35.4 cm

5   37 cm

5   37 cm

5   34.2 cm

5   27.6 cm

5

Fig. 6 Measurements for the shape of the lid.

Fold and pin the inside corners of the lid, mirroring the placement on the sketch. The rear folds should be roughly 8 cm deep and slightly wider than the front ones, which are 7 cm deep. The depth and placement of these folds will determine the shape of the curved lid. Test out the shape on your backpack once you have pinned each corner, and adjust as necessary. The lid should cover the entire top of the backpack when full. It is sewn on at the back, roughly 2 cm beneath the lower edge of the hem.

When you're happy with the shape of the lid, sew the folds, cut away any excess material, and press in the edges.

Press a 6 mm fold around the edge of the lid. Clip this fold wherever you need to, to avoid any creases, then glue the fold against the inside of the lid.

Sew bias binding around the entire edge of the lid so that the glued fold is hidden. The purpose of the folding in the previous step is to make the edges of the lid a little sturdier.

Fit the lid to the backpack so that it is centred and adequately low at the back. Sew it into place through the edging strip using two parallel seams 8 mm apart.

FASTENINGS

The last step is to cut out the leather to fasten the bag. I've chosen to have one long strap to hold the bag closed; that way, you can store a rolled up sleeping mat beneath the lid, even when the backpack is almost full. You can choose to use a shorter strap if you don't have that requirement.

Cut out a leather strap measuring roughly 37 cm in length, round the corners and narrow the tip slightly by cutting away narrow wedges 3 cm from the end. Use an awl to mark out the placement of 7 holes for the buckle, at the following distances from the tip: 7, 10, 13, 16, 19, 22 and 25 cm – i.e. with a distance of 3 cm between each hole.

Next, mark out the holes for attaching the strap to the lid at the following distances from the other end: 1.5, 5.5 and 8 cm.

Use a hole punch to make the holes you marked out for fastening the strap to the lid. Take care to make sure that the holes are in the very centre of the strap; it will be very visible if they aren't, which isn't a good look.

Lastly, make the 7 holes for the buckle.

Cut out an 85 × 20 mm piece of leather to sit beneath the rivets on the inside of the lid. Mark and make the same rivet holes as on the strap.

Fit the strap to the lid. First, mark the centre point of the lid and then line up the strap vertically against it. I decided to place the back end of the strap 11 cm from the edge of the lid.

Mark out the position of the holes with an awl and pierce the lid. Fasten everything together with three 10 mm rivets.

Cut out a 120 × 20 mm leather strap to hold the buckle in place (see Fig. 7).

Mark the middle of the strap with the awl and then, on its centre line, mark the placement of a 3 mm wide and 16 mm long hole in the middle of the strap (lengthwise).

Use the hole punch to make two holes at each end of this, then cut out the leather between the two holes, forming a larger gap. You'll have to use a penknife or Stanley knife against a ruler here, because the rotary cutter won't be able to make such a short cut.

Fold the strap in half. Mark the holes for the rivets at 1.5 and 4.5 cm from the folded edge, respectively. Line up the ends of the strap and make the holes for the rivets – 2 squeezes of the hole punch will make 4 holes.

Cut a 55 × 20 mm piece of leather to sit beneath the rivets on the inside of the bag, and punch the same holes in it.

Place the leather strap with the buckle threaded onto it vertically between the pockets on the front of the bag, in such a position that the lid can close nicely when the bag is both full or half-full, and even with a sleeping mat beneath the lid.

Mark out the rivet holes and punch a hole in the front of the bag using the awl – you won't be able to use the hole punch here. Attach the strap to the front of the backpack using two 10 mm rivets. Choose the right size

Fig. 7 Leather strap for holding the buckle in place.

A

B

C

D

E

F

G

H

I

R

S

J

Q

T

U

K

L

M

N

O

P ●

X

V

Y Z AA BB

W

62

for the holes you have made so that the rivets fit the hole perfectly; too large a hole will have a negative effect on durability.

STRAP ENDINGS

Finally, thread the webbing straps from the triangles through the plastic buckles on the shoulder straps.

Cut out two 80 × 20 mm pieces of leather, fold them in the middle lengthwise and sew them over the end of the polyester webbing; mark out lines 3 mm from the edge on the leather, and sew by turning the hand wheel on the machine.

PROJECT COMPONENTS

A Main body, outer material, 72 × 55 cm (× 1)

B Back piece, outer material, 33 × 55 cm (× 1)

C Back piece, liner material, 33 × 47 cm (× 1)

D Back piece, padding material, 29 × 35 cm (× 1)

E Reinforcement for back piece, outer material, 33 × 22 cm (× 1)

F Bottom piece, outer material, 31.5 × 23 cm, radius 10 cm (× 1)

G Bottom piece, liner material, 31.5 × 23 cm, radius 10 cm (× 1)

H Bottom piece, padding material, 30 × 21.5 cm, radius 10 cm (× 1)

I Pocket for inside of back piece, liner material, 24 × 28 cm (× 1)

J Pocket for outside of main body, outer material, 27 × 33 cm (× 2)

K Zip, size 5, 24 cm (× 2)

L Polyester webbing strap, 6 cm × 20 mm (× 2)

M Polyester webbing strap, 37 cm × 20 mm (× 2)

N End piece, 2 mm leather, 80 × 20 mm (× 2)

O Strap for attaching strap adjusters, 2 mm leather, 20 × 180 mm (× 2)

P Back piece for rivets, 2 mm leather, 18 mm diameter (× 4)

Q Lid, outer material, measurements according to drawing (× 1)

R Shoulder straps, outer material, measurement according to drawing, seam allowance of 15 mm to be added around edge if drawing is of actual size (× 4)

S Foam for shoulder straps, 1–2 mm thick foam, measurement according to drawing, no seam allowance to be added (× 4)

T Carry handle, outer material, 28 × 6 cm (× 1)

U Fabric for sewing shoulder straps to back piece, outer material, 33 × 8 cm (× 1)

V Shoulder strap triangles, outer fabric, base = 24 cm, height = 12 cm (× 2)

W Leather cord, 125 cm (× 1)

X Edging for lid, bias binding, 100 cm × 30 mm (× 1)

Y Fastening strap, 2 mm leather, 370 × 20 mm (× 1)

Z Back piece for rivets, 2 mm leather, 85 × 20 mm (× 1)

AA Strap for buckle, 2 mm leather, 120 × 20 mm (× 1)

BB Back piece for rivets, 2 mm leather, 55 × 20 mm (× 1)

GAITERS

TIME: 6 HOURS | LEVEL 3

A good pair of gaiters will keep the snow out of
your boots and trousers. Many trousers designed
for downhill skiing come with internal gaiter cuffs,
but I prefer to ski in ordinary walking trousers that I
can wear all year round. They might have adjustable
straps around the ankles, but they let in a lot of snow
all the same. With a pair of gaiters, you can ski in
knee-deep powder snow without getting any in
your boots.

SEWING THE ELASTIC INTO THE MATERIAL

MATERIAL

- densely woven
  fabric (i.e. poplin),
  c.60 cm × 1 metre
- elastic, c.3 metres,
  6–10 mm width
- 2 mm leather,
  c.12 × 4.5 cm
- 1 mm leather, c.5 × 5 cm
- binding wire, 20 cm,
  c.1.5 mm thickness
- polyester webbing,
  1 metre, 20 mm width
- 2 sturdy press studs

Measure and cut out two pieces of fabric, 54 × 46 cm.

Measure out two 36 cm lengths of elastic for the 'waist', which will sit
on the inside of the gaiter, level with the cuff of your boot. The elastic will
be sewn into place straight across the material's 46 cm side.

Using a felt tip, mark the two pieces of elastic 2 cm from each end. On
the material, mark the elastic's position 19 cm from the lower edge of the
fabric, and draw a line there using tailor's chalk.

Stretch out and pin the elastic evenly across the fabric. The trick is
to line up and pin the marks you drew on the elastic with the edge of
the material, and then to stretch out the material on a table and pin the
elastic to it – the material will be flat, which will make it easier to pin the
entire length of elastic. You should be left with 2 cm of elastic overhang-
ing both sides of the material. This is only there to hold on to while you
sew, and will be cut off later.

Sew the elastic to the material using a straight stitch, lengthwise down
the middle of the elastic. The stitch length should be 4 mm. This can be a bit
tricky: you need to stretch out the elastic so that the material is entirely flat
as you sew. Begin by securing the thread at one end, then take hold of the
elastic behind the machine and stretch the material and elastic backwards

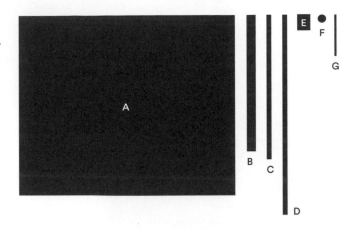

A Main body, outer fabric,
   54 × 46 cm (× 2)

B Foot strap, polyester
   webbing, 30 cm ×
   20 mm (× 2)

C Waist, 6 mm elastic,
   36 cm (× 2)

D Hem elastic, 6 mm
   elastic, 50 cm (× 4)

E Leather flap, 2 mm
   leather, 30 × 45 mm
   (× 4)

F Back piece for rivets,
   1 mm leather, 18 mm
   diameter (× 6)

G Shoe hook, binding
   wire, 10 cm (× 2)

as you gently pull the entire piece forward, helping the machine to feed the material forward as you sew. Finish off by securing the thread. The elastic should be evenly affixed to the material now, forming a wavy line. Repeat with the other piece of fabric.

SEW CYLINDERS FROM THE PIECES OF FABRIC

Fold the piece of material with the elastic sewn onto it in the middle, and pin it so that it forms a cylinder. The elastic should be visible on the outside as you sew.

Sew along the 54 cm edge with a seam allowance of roughly 12 mm; when you are finished, the piece of fabric should resemble a tube. If you like, you can also sew some bias binding over the seams to achieve a more attractive inside. This isn't necessary, however, so I have skipped this step.

HEMMING AND THREADING IN THE ELASTIC

Hem the gaiters at the top and bottom; the elastic will be threaded into these hems later.

Fold and press a 2.2 cm hem at both the top and bottom of the tube – i.e. first fold a 2 cm hem, press it, then fold the edge again, and press. Secure with a couple of pins to make sure the hems are even.

Sew each hem twice. One row of stitching should be 3 mm from the fold and the other 3 mm from the loose edge. Leave a 2 cm gap between where you begin and end your stitches. This will allow you to thread the elastic into the hems later. Repeat the process with the bottom hem.

Thread 50 cm of elastic onto a safety needle, pull the elastic through the

Fig. 1 Placement of
the lower (front) and
upper (back) flaps.

hem and tie loosely. Check that the elastic is tight enough; the upper elastic should hold the gaiter up at your knee and should not be too tight. At the bottom, the elastic should be suitably tight around the cuff of your boot. When you're happy with the elastic, tighten the knots and sew up the small openings in both the upper and lower hems.

LEATHER FLAPS

These pieces of leather will sit at the very bottom on the front of the gaiters, hiding the boot hooks, and at the very top at the back, acting as pull flaps. Cut four pieces of leather measuring 30 × 45 mm and round off the corners.

Use an awl to mark a faint line dividing the pieces of leather in two (at the mid-point of the 45 mm sides). Taking the centre line as your starting point, use an awl to draw 4 guide lines roughly 3 mm from the edge, forming a rectangle. You will be able to sew on the pieces of leather using these lines later.

The (vertical) seam on the fabric tube should be centred at the back, meaning that the lower piece of leather should be on the bottom hem on the opposite side, and that the upper piece of leather should be at the back, right on top of the seam (see Fig. 1).

Glue half of the leather onto the material. The glue-free part should be loose, a kind of flap you can hold onto. Apply contact adhesive to both the fabric and the leather and allow to dry for around 5 minutes, until it no longer feels tacky. The piece of leather for the bottom hem should be left unglued in the middle, where the boot hooks will sit later. Only glue this piece around the edges, in other words.

Sew the pieces of leather into place as slowly as you can on the machine, using the hand wheel to help it along. Try to follow the lines you drew precisely, and when you turn the corner it is important that the needle goes down at the exact point the guide lines meet, in order to achieve a nice angle. The lower piece of leather should be sewn along three edges: the bottom edge is left open. This is where the boot hooks will be stuck in.

BOOT HOOKS

Use the binding wire to make two boot hooks, following steps 1–6 in Fig. 2. Cut a 10 cm length of binding wire and make sure it is completely straight. Next, bend it carefully, step by step. It's a bit fiddly, but it can be done. The wire will become firm with the many bends you make, so

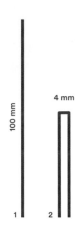

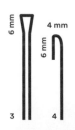

Fig. 2 Steps for bending the boot hooks.

it won't straighten out. A small, sturdy pair of flat-nosed pliers will work well for bending the wire.

Lastly, place a hook on top of the lower piece of leather so that it sticks out 10 mm over the edge. Mark 6 small holes with the awl. Check that the holes are nice and symmetrical, then punch the awl through the leather. Push the hook between the leather and the material and sew the hook into place with 2 + 2 + 2 hand stitches. Repeat on the second gaiter.

FOOT STRAP

To stop the gaiter from riding up on the cuff of the boot, you should attach a strap which runs from the inner bottom edge, beneath the sole of the boot by the heel, and up to the outer edge of the opposite side, where it is fastened with a press stud. Try on your gaiters with the boots you want to use them with, and measure out a suitable length of strap from the polyester webbing. Mine was 30 cm.

Cut 2 pieces of strap at the right length and use a lighter to burn the cut ends, to prevent them from fraying.

Sew the strap onto the inner lower edge with a square seam with a cross inside it (a so-called 'X box').

Cut out 6 leather circles with a diameter of roughly 18 mm; these are primarily added as reinforcements beneath the press-studs, but also because they look good. There are special leather tools, so-called punches, for cutting out perfect circles, but they are quite expensive, and if the leather isn't too thick it works just as well to draw the circle with an awl and then cut it out. I tend to use a coin with the right diameter as an outline.

Punch a hole in the middle of each leather circle using a hole punch. The hole should be the same size as the 'tube' in the middle of the press-stud. You should also make a hole on the bottom hem of the gaiter, on the opposite side to where the strap has been attached, as well as in the loose end of the strap. I folded the end of the strap back on itself and punched a hole in both sides to achieve a thick enough material for the press-stud. Attach the press-studs and the leather circles using the press stud tool. Hit firmly but not too hard with the hammer when fitting the press-studs.

FIREWOOD HOLDER

TIME: 6 HOURS | LEVEL 2.5

A simple, sturdy log holder for carrying wood to the sauna or the wood-fired oven. It looks good, doesn't take long to sew, and doesn't take up space when you aren't using it. It's also a great gift and a perfect introduction to heavy-duty sewing.

THE MAIN BODY

Cut out a piece of outer material measuring 100 × 37 cm.

Press a 12 mm wide hem along each of the long sides, and sew this into place 3 mm from the inner edge. Roughly 6 cm from both ends, cut away the inner fold of the hem. This will mean you have fewer layers to sew through when hemming the short sides.

Press the hems on the short sides by first folding in 15 mm and then another 30 mm – leaving you with a 30 mm wide hem. Sew along both edges of the hem, 3 mm from each edge.

LEATHER HANDLES

I used a 2 mm vegetable-tanned, non-dyed (natural coloured) leather for the handles.

With an awl, draw on the leather and cut out two 3 × 38 cm pieces. Round off the corners using a chisel.

Measure out and use the awl to mark the mid-point of the leather, as well as 9 cm from the middle in each direction. Next, use the tracing wheel to draw an 18 cm line along both sides of the handle, roughly 3 mm from the edge. Try to start with the wheel in the same position on both the upper and lower line, so that the holes on the handle line up.

Use the awl to punch holes in the leather. I make holes in every other mark made by the tracing wheel, which gives me a distance of 5 mm between holes. This will look good when hand sewn with thick, waxed thread. Check that you have an equal number of holes on both lines.

MATERIAL

- densely woven polyester/ cotton canvas outer material, 100 × 37 cm
- 2 mm leather straps, 2 × 60 cm (× 1) and 3 × 80 cm (× 2)
- waxed linen thread, c.120 cm
- rivets, 10 mm (× 4)
- metal D rings, 25 mm (× 2)

73

Thread a needle onto both ends of a waxed linen thread, and sew by hand in line with the instructions for hand sewing on p. 45. Finish off by securing the threads before you cut them.

SEWING THE HANDLES ONTO THE FIREWOOD HOLDER

Use the awl to draw the lines you want your stitches to follow. To ensure that these visible stitches look good, you need a guide line to follow. I chose a 20 × 20 square of stitches, 3 mm from the edge.

On the hems of the main body, mark where the centre point is. There should be a distance of 14 cm between the two sides of each handle on the firewood holder, so measure out and make a mark 7 cm from the middle in each direction. This will be the position for the middle of your handles.

Place the handles so that they are centred on the markings, and draw around the outer edge of the handle. Apply a thin layer of contact adhesive to the leather and the fabric, leave to dry for five minutes, place the handles in the right position and press down. This will make it easier to sew them into the right position using a sewing machine, without them moving off centre.

Start by sewing the upper seam and turn by 90 degrees at each corner. Take care when you make your first stitch that you finish precisely in a corner. Drive the machine by hand, using the hand wheel, and pay attention to where the needle is going down, to make sure you are always following your markings. As you approach the end of each row of stitches, adjust the length of the last stitch so that the needle neatly fits the corner where you want to turn by 90 degrees. Lastly, sew over the last stitch twice, forward and back, both to reinforce the seam and to secure the thread. Do the same with the handle on the opposite side.

FASTENING

Cut a 41 × 2 cm leather strap. Also cut out two pieces measuring 3 × 2 cm, and one measuring 10 × 2 cm.

Narrow one end of the long strap slightly, roughly 3 cm from the end, and round off all corners using a chisel.

Measure out, use the awl to mark, and then punch two holes in the other end of the long strap, 10 and 25 mm from the edge.

Punch holes into the same places on the 3 × 2 cm pieces, which will sit beneath the rivets on the other side of the fabric, as well as on the 10 cm piece (which should be folded in half). It needs four holes, since it will be wound around the two D rings and riveted into place.

The same holes should be punched into the centre line of the upper seam on both sides of the main body.

Use a hole punch for all of the holes, and rivet the long strap into place on one side, the short strap holding the D rings onto the other. This means that the firewood holder can be strapped shut by first threading the strap through both rings and then back through the inner ring.

TOTE BAG

TIME: 6 HOURS | LEVEL 3

A tote bag is the simplest kind of bag, essentially a fabric bucket with handles, and often without fastenings of any kind. The original is generally considered to be the 'boat bag', designed by American clothing company L. L. Bean, which was launched in 1944. The tote is an incredibly functional bag given that it is easy to access and has a fairly large volume. I've chosen to sew an open, slightly larger variant, with short handles. It's perfect for shopping or for shoving a couple of towels, a pair of swimming trunks and a bottle of juice into when you're going swimming.

MATERIAL

- densely woven polyester/cotton canvas outer material, *c.*150 × 60 cm
- cotton/polyester poplin lining, *c.*40 × 25 cm
- bias binding, 30 mm wide, *c.*120 cm
- sleeping pad for padding, 4 mm thickness, *c.*40 × 25 cm
- coil zip with one slider, size 5, 25 cm
- leather strap, 2 mm thickness, 3 × 80 cm
- waxed linen thread, *c.*120 cm

CUT OUT THE PIECES

The bottom piece should measure 38 × 21 cm, including a 1.5 cm seam allowance around the edges. Measure, draw and cut out a piece of outer material and liner to these measurements, as well as a piece of padding measuring 35 × 18 cm.

Glue the padding in the centre of the outer material using a thin layer of contact adhesive.

Cut out the main body from the outer material, which measures 112 × 50 cm, and a pocket measuring 46 × 26 cm.

SEW THE POCKET

The pocket has a zip sewn into place using the method illustrated on page 57.

Begin by drawing the 21 cm line that will form the hole for the zip. This should be 5 cm beneath one of the short edges of the piece of fabric. Next, cut the line, press back the edges, pin the zip into place, and sew around the edges.

Sew straight over the zip at both ends. Cut away any excess zip and hold the lighter to the ends to prevent them from fraying.

Fold the fabric in the middle so that the zip is on the inside, then sew around the edges to form a flat pouch. Turn it the right way out, and your pocket is now ready to sew onto the bag.

SEW TOGETHER THE BOTTOM AND THE MAIN BODY

Pin the bottom to the main body, with the wrong side of the fabric facing out. The side seam of the main body should be centred on one of the short sides of the base.

Mark where the seam on the main body should sit to make sure that the two pieces are lined up. They should both have the same circumference, so you will be able to pin them without any creases.

Take out the pins and sew the side seam on the main body. Cut away any excess fabric to form a straight, even, lower edge.

Pin the bottom to the main body once again, and sew the two pieces together with a seam allowance of *c.*12 mm. Check that there are no creases at the corners.

Sew an extra row of stitches on top of the existing stitches at each corner. Since the corners will be subject to a substantial amount of wear, this will act as a reinforcement.

Trim the seam allowance so that you are left with only 1 cm of fabric, and sew binding around the seams on the base. If you like, you can also sew bias binding onto the side seam of the main body.

Turn the bag the right way out and push out the corners properly. Fold down the top of the bag by 2 cm and press. Now, fold another 5 cm and press. You should be left with a top hem of roughly 5 cm.

Place the hanging pocket in the centre of one side so that the hem is overlapping it by *c.*3 cm. Pin in a few places so that both the hem and the pocket stay put.

On the outside of the bag, use tailor's chalk and a ruler to mark where you want the row of stitches to be.

Sew from the outside of the bag so that the more attractive upper thread is visible. Use *c.*3.5 mm stitches and take care to make sure your seam is neat.

HANDLES

To sew the handles into place, follow the same instructions as for the firewood holder on page 74, with the difference that there should be a 13 cm gap between the two ends of each handle on the tote bag, and that they should be sewn into position with the ends of the handles lined up with the edge of the hems.

The handles should be sewn onto the hem using rectangular seams measuring 20 × 35 mm.

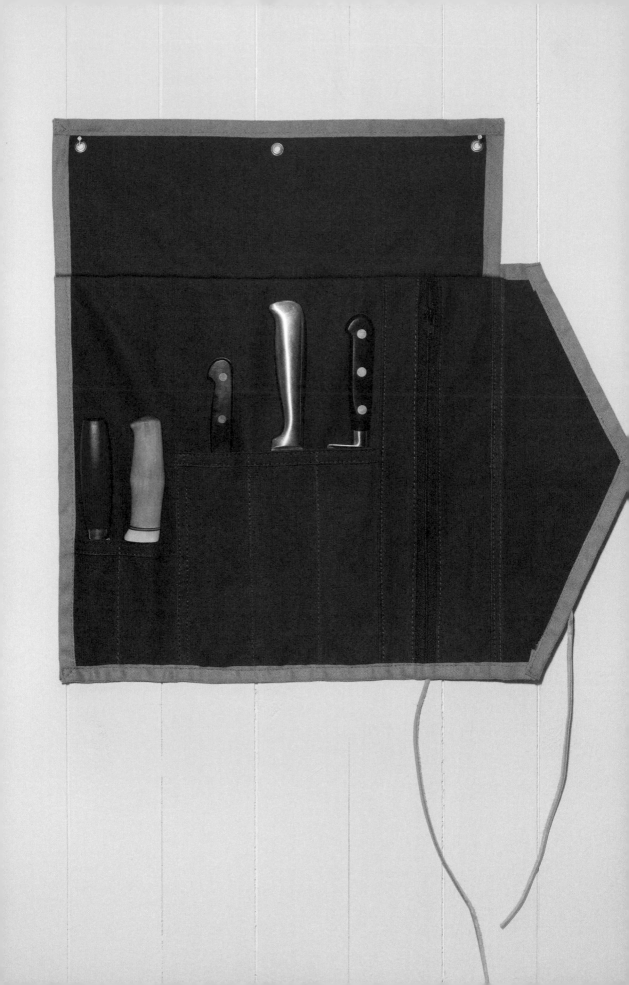

KNIFE POUCH

TIME: 5 HOURS | LEVEL 2

This pouch is for kitchen knives and other tools, making it easy for you to carry your favourites with you. I chose to make a smallish pouch with space for three large and two small knives, as well as a zipped pocket for smaller objects, but you can follow the same principles to make a larger pouch for more knives. Using the same design at a larger scale also makes a great tool holder. The knife pouch can be rolled up and tied shut with a leather strap. In its unrolled state, you can hang it from the wall using the eyelets.

MATERIAL

– densely woven polyester/
  cotton canvas outer
  material, c. 50 × 150 cm
– coil zip with one
  slider, size 5, 40 cm
– bias binding, 30 mm
  width, c. 2.5 metres
– eyelets, 10 mm (× 3)
– leather cord, 100 cm

SEW THE BODY, THE POCKETS AND THE KNIFE POUCHES

Cut out the large piece of outer material that will form the body of your pouch. It should measure 60 × 37 cm.

Mark the mid point on the right-hand short side, then make a mark 8 cm from the right hand side on the two longer edges. Taking these markers, use a ruler to draw the triangle that will form the right hand side of the pouch. Cut away the material to the right of your markings so that you are left with a triangle.

Cut out the outer material for the pocket which will have a zip running its entire length; the material should be 13 × 37 cm, which will leave you with a 10 cm wide pocket.

Next, cut the piece of fabric for the pocket lengthways, so that you end up with two pieces: they should be 5 cm and 8 cm wide, respectively. Press a fold of 1 cm along the edge of the 8 × 37 cm piece, and sew the zip into place along the entire length.

Press a fold of 1 cm along the other piece, and sew the other side of the zip into place. Sew roughly 3 mm from the folded edge of the material, taking care to make sure you have a nice, straight seam and that the visible section of zip is the same width all the way along. Around 18 mm is a suitable width for the zip.

Sew the pocket into place on the main body by pressing 13 cm of the triangular flap over the main body, then folding 12 cm of it back on itself. Position the zipped pocket beneath the 1 cm fold that has been created at the base of the triangle, and pin into place.

Sew the pocket to the main body with two parallel seams, one along the folded edge on the inside, and one along the folded edge on the outside. For the sake of ease, sew one row of stitches with the inside up and the other with the outside up. Next, press a 1 cm hem along the free long edge of the pocket.

Cut the outer material for the large knife pouch, 21 × 22.5 cm. Press the upper edge along the 21 cm side, first by *c.*5 mm and then by 12 mm, so that you are left with a 12 mm hem.

Sew a seam along the upper part of this hem, 3 mm from the edge, and another along the lower part, so that you have two parallel seams forming the upper edge of the pouch.

Pin the material beneath the hem you pressed on the pocket, and sew the zipped pocket and the knife pouch to the main body using a seam which

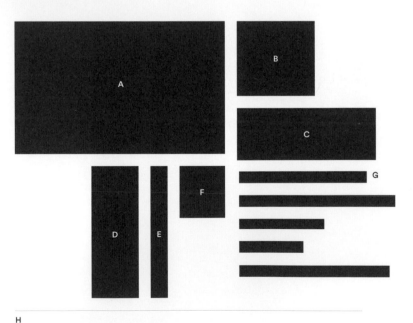

82

runs parallel to the zip. Sew the seam for the knife pouch twice, ideally in the same needle holes if you can. Begin from the top and sew all the way down. Turn by 180 degrees and sew until you have passed the top edge of the knife pouch and finished off with a short forward and backstitch. These double seams will be more resistant to the sharp tips of the knives, which, over time, risk wearing through the thread in the seams.

Cut out a piece of outer material for the small knife pouch, 12.5 × 15 cm. Sew a double seam hem along the 12.5 cm edge in the same way you did for the large pouch.

Press a 1 cm hem along the loose edge of the large pouch, and allow this to overlap the small pouch by 1 cm. Sew both into place with a double, parallel seam. Sew everything twice to produce an extra strong seam for the knives.

Sew the row of stitches that divides the small knife pouch into two, roughly 5 cm from the edge of the larger pouch. Sew from the bottom up, over the hemmed edge and back down again, producing a double seam.

Sew the two rows of stitches that divide the large knife pouch into three. I made the right hand pouch 5 cm wide and the two to the left 6 cm. Sew from the bottom up, over the hemmed edge and back down again, producing double seams.

Cut out a 15 × 40 cm piece of outer material. This will be the lid which folds down over the pouch to stop the knives from falling out. This is also where the eyelets will be.

Cut 3 lengths of bias binding, two measuring 15 cm and one measuring 43 cm.

Sew the binding onto the short sides of the lid first, and then along the upper long edge, which will cover the ends of the binding on the short sides.

Fold in the ends of the upper length of binding so that it lines up with the side strips, and finish off with a small triangle seam.

EDGING AND EYELETS

All of the sections of the knife pouch are now ready, and all that remains is to sew bias binding around the main body. This edging will also secure the flap to the main body. The binding should be sewn with the inside of the pouch facing up; that way, the visible seams will also be the most attractive.

First, neaten up the entire pouch so that the edges are straight. It should measure 36 × 40 cm, plus the triangular flap.

Take the bias binding and use an iron to press it in the middle, leaving

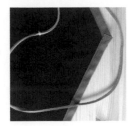

Fig. 1 Finishing stitches on bias binding and attachment of leather cord.

it folded in half lengthwise. Make sure the fold is in the exact middle (the strip will be sewn roughly 3 mm from the edge, and if the fold is in the very middle then the lower stitches will also be 3 mm from the edge if you have pinned everything carefully).

Measure out appropriate lengths of bias binding for each side of the pouch, and add an extra 2 cm to each end.

Begin with the lower edge. Fold in the ends of the binding and pin to the pouch. Sew the bottom seam twice (forward and back) and use shorter stitches, roughly 2 mm, so that the stitching withstands the tips of the knives. Continue this way with the binding on the left hand side.

Place the piece of material for the lid (which already has edging along 3 of its 4 sides) into position on top of the pouch, and pin it into place with the bias binding on top. Fold in the end (c. 1–2 cm) of the bias binding at the left hand side. On the right, cut off the bias binding where the pouch stops. Sew the pieces together 3 mm from the lower edge of the bias binding.

Finally, sew the edging onto the triangular flap. Since the triangular flap is most visible when the pouch is rolled up, I chose to turn the entire piece upside down to sew the binding from the outside – in order to have the most attractive stitching visible there. Cut two pieces of binding, 25 cm each. Pin the first into place and sew on. To achieve a neat look at the tip of the triangle, I glue the last piece of binding onto the material before I start sewing; this way, it stays in position. The bias binding will meet at the tip of the triangle, where I sew an additional finishing stitch (see Fig. 1).

Now, use a hole punch to make 3 holes in the flap, roughly 1 cm beneath the binding – one in each corner and one in the middle. Attach the eyelets. These can be used to hang the knife pouch on the wall.

LEATHER FASTENING

Mark out a suitable position for the leather cord that you will use to tie the pouch when it is rolled up. You'll need roughly 1 metre of leather.

To do this, fill the pouch with knives and then roll it up and tie the leather cord around it.

Mark out a suitable position to sew the cord to the pouch. I placed mine right next to the seam along the triangular flap (see Fig. 1). I hand sewed 4–5 times around the leather cord. The placement of these hand stitches means that the inside of the stitching is hidden inside the zipped pocket, and is not visible on the inside of the pouch.

APRON

TIME: 5 HOURS | LEVEL 2

This apron is based on a model designed by chef Niklas Ekstedt in collaboration with Sandqvist. I chose to use a slightly thinner material than the thick canvas Sandqvist uses, in order to make the apron slightly more comfortable. I've also angled the neck strap slightly, and made it fixed instead of adjustable. It's an attractive and practical apron for barbecuing, general cookery, even tinkering about in the garage. The sewing is relatively simple and the leatherwork is quick to do. As a sewing project, it's a great way to fill your spare time.

MATERIAL

- densely-woven polyester/ cotton canvas outer material, c.71 × 150 cm
- leather for neck strap, 2 mm thickness, 64 cm × 16 mm
- leather for waist tie, 2 mm thickness, 64 cm × 16 mm
- leather strap for D rings, 2 mm thickness, 15 cm × 16 mm
- leather pieces (× 3), 2 mm thickness, 7 cm × 16 mm
- rivets, 6 mm (× 8)
- metal D ring, c.20 mm (× 2)

CUT OUT THE BODY AND HEM THE EDGES

Cut out the material for the apron according to the pattern on p. 89. Since the pattern shows a ready-hemmed apron, remember to add a 15 mm seam allowance on each side. Begin with a rectangle measuring 86 × 68 cm and then draw in the curves where the apron narrows towards the top. Use cups and plates of the appropriate size to find the right radius. It's better to cut away too little to begin with, so that you can try on the apron and adjust.

The apron has rounded corners, which can be quite tricky to achieve when sewing a relatively thick fabric. You can't just fold a hem and sew it the way you would a rectangular piece of fabric; instead, you need to clip the folded fabric to prevent it from bunching up and becoming too thick on the curve (see Fig. 1). Clip four incisions on each rounded corner. Do a test run with a piece of paper before you cut the fabric to check how large these incisions need to be, and to check which angle they need to be at to achieve a neat curve.

Press a 12 mm hem (fold over 5 mm first, then another 12 mm) around the entire apron, and pin into place. I like to glue the hem at the corners, which helps to keep it in place as I sew. Just remember to use as little glue as possible on the corners, to prevent the needle from sticking as you sew through it.

Sew a double hem around the apron: one row of stitches 2–3 mm from the inner edge of the hem and one 2 mm from the outer edge of the apron. The side on which the hem is visible (upwards) is the inside of the apron. I tend to sew the along the inside of the hem first – with the inside of the apron facing up. The better you have pinned the hem and managed to get it exactly 1 cm wide all the way around, the better the double rows of stitches will look. If the hem varies in width between, say, 8 and 15 mm, then the distance between the two seams will also vary.

Next, turn over the apron so that the outside is facing upwards on the machine, and sew the second row of stitches around the outer edge of the apron.

POCKETS

Cut out the material for the pockets. The apron should have two large pockets at the waist and a smaller pen pocket on the chest. The measurements are 14 × 11 cm for the pen pocket and 22 × 24 cm for the two larger pockets.

Trim the upper edges of the larger pockets so that they are angled slightly (measure 5 cm from the upper edge at one side, draw a line to the opposite corner and cut).

Fold and press 15 mm of the upper edge on all 3 pockets to create simple, one-fold hems. Secure this with double, parallel rows of stitching with roughly 8 mm between the two.

Next, press simple hems of roughly 10 mm around the sides and bottoms of each pocket, and pin them into place on the apron. I chose to position the two large pockets 19 cm from the lower edge of the apron and 6 cm from the sides. I placed the pen pocket so that its lower edge is 17.5 cm beneath the top of the apron and 4 cm from the edge. Pinning these into place before you start to sew allows you test out the positions to see what suits you. Once you're happy, sew each pocket into place. Begin and end with forward and backstitches.

A Main body, outer
   material, 71 × 89 cm (× 1)

B Waist strap, 2 mm
   leather, 65 cm × 16 mm
   (× 1)

C Neck strap, 2 mm
   leather, 65 cm × 16 mm
   (× 1)

D Large pockets, outer
   material, 22 × 24 cm
   (× 2)

E Pen pocket, outer
   material, 14 × 11 cm (× 1)

F Back piece for
   rivets, 2 mm leather,
   7 cm × 16 mm (× 3)

G D-ring holder, 2 mm
   leather, 15 cm × 16 mm
   (× 1)

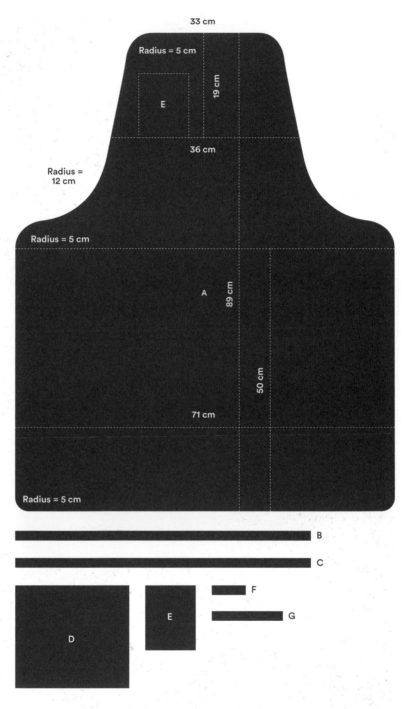

Fig. 1 Rounded corners
and the leather rivet piece
on the back of the apron.

Cut out the straps from a larger skin or use ready-cut leather straps. Round off all the corners.

Take the neck strap and punch holes for the rivets (with a diameter of 15 mm) 55 mm from the ends. Punch mirroring holes into all 3 pieces of leather that will sit beneath the rivets on the reverse of the apron.

Place the neck strap on top of the apron so that its ends overlap the fabric by c.8 cm and so that the distance between the ends on the top line is c.20–21 cm. They should be angled gently outwards, which will help the strap to feel comfortable around your neck. Play around with the angle to work out what suits you best.

Mark and punch the necessary holes in the apron, then rivet the neck strap into place with two pieces of leather on the reverse (see Fig. 1).

Try on the apron and measure where you want the waist strap to sit. Mine ended up being c.4 cm beneath where the apron starts to narrow – i.e. 47.5 cm from the lower edge of the apron.

Fold the strap which will hold the D rings in the middle, mark out where the holes should be, and punch them through the leather. I chose to make the first hole 15 mm from the ends and the second 55 mm from the ends.

Draw onto the apron where you will punch the corresponding holes, then use the hole punch to do so.

Thread the D rings onto the leather and rivet the leather strap into place so that one half is on the front of the apron and the other on the back. The D rings should sit right by the edge of the apron.

Punch the same holes into the longer leather strap, mark out the holes on the fabric, punch the holes and then rivet this final strap into place, with the back piece on the reverse.

DUFFEL BAG

TIME: 10 HOURS | LEVEL 3

A classic duffel bag has only one opening, at the top of the cylinder, which makes it virtually impossible to get to anything at the bottom. That's why I've made an updated version, which has a zip opening right down its length and even across one of the ends. It means the bag opens right up, so you can more easily access your things. My version is adapted to fit on my motorbike, but you can obviously choose different measurements and details to meet your specific needs. This project can easily be adjusted to make a bag suitable for carrying a yoga mat, for example, or for carrying gym kit.

MATERIAL

- densely woven polyester/cotton canvas outer material, c. 100 × 150 cm
- coil zip with 4 sliders, size 5, 160 cm
- leather strap, 2 mm thickness, 30 mm width, c. 80 cm length

CALCULATE THE SIZE OF THE PIECES

Sewing two circular end pieces to a rectangle in order to form a cylinder requires a little planning and care to get right. I wanted the finished product to measure 61 × 31 cm (the diameter of the sides), which would give a volume of 46 litres. The end pieces need to be 34 cm in diameter, which gives a 15 mm seam allowance around their circumference. When the main body is sewn to the end pieces, it will follow a circle with a 31 cm diameter – i.e. the seam allowance at the edges will be folded in. According to the formula 31 × 3.14 cm, the main body should therefore be around 97 cm wide (a circle's circumference is calculated as D × 3.14). However, the zip is 18 mm wide when sewn into place, and the main body requires a seam allowance of 15 mm at each side of the zip.

To avoid the risk that the main body is too short to fully wrap around the circular end pieces, I increased the seam allowance to 25 mm. As a result, the main body is 100.5 cm wide (31 × 3.14 + 2.5 + 2.5 − 1.8 = 100.5 cm), and 61 + 3 cm in height.

93

If you want to make your bag to different measurements, begin by deciding on the final length (L) and diameter (D), and calculate how big your main body should be using the following formula: $D \times 3.14 + 2.5 + 2.5 - 1.8$. The diameter of the end pieces should be cut to $D + 3$ cm. The main body should be $L + 3$.

94

Find a large serving plate with a diameter of 34 cm and draw two circles onto the fabric.

Cut out the circles and take care to make sure they are both exactly the same size, as this will make things easier once they are sewn to the main body.

Cut out the main body, which should measure 64 × 100.5 cm. Fold and press a 1.5 cm hem on both of the long edges. The width of these folds may need to be adjusted after you have pinned the main body to the end pieces.

OUTER POCKET

I wanted my duffel bag to have a small outside pocket large enough to keep bits and pieces in. Since a flat outer pocket is difficult to get into when the bag is fully packed, a pocket with its own volume works better. I often strap the bag onto my motorcycle, but I wanted to be able to get at the pocket even when the bag is strapped on. In other words, I wanted to be able to open the pocket without the contents falling out, both when the bag is on its end and when it's being carried horizontally in my hand. That meant a certain amount of thought about the placement of the zip.

Cut out a 16 × 21 cm piece of material and round the corners using, for example, a tea cup.

Cut out a strip of material measuring 4 × 42 cm, followed by a 28 cm length of zip.

Fold and press 1 cm of fabric at the end of the strip of material, position the material over the end of the zip so that their centre lines meet, then sew them together to form one long strip.

Pin the material + zip to the side of the 16 × 21 piece of fabric, and sew them together along the edge of the strip. Sew the ends of the strip together so that it forms a frame around the pocket. Make sure the opening of the zip is pointing the right way in relation to how the pocket will be attached to the bag.

Turn the pocket the right way out and press a small 5–7 mm fold inwards around the entire edge of the frame. Next, position the pocket on the bag (the main body), centred laterally and roughly 13 cm beneath the hemmed edge.

Pin the small hem inwards, against the bag, and sew around the pocket, roughly 2 mm from the edge. This can be quite tricky with such a small hem and such sharp corners, but if you take your time it should be fine. If it goes wrong, just unpick, take a break and start again.

Cut out a 30 × 34 cm piece of material, a 34 cm length of zip and a strip of material measuring 6 × 34 cm.

Press a hem on both pieces of material, and sew the zip between the two to form a flat pocket.

Cut two 30 cm lengths of bias binding and press them in the middle. Sew these into place on the right and left hand sides of the pocket, so that the edges of the fabric and the ends of the zip are hidden.

Press hems of 1 cm on the upper and lower edges of the pocket.

Pin the pocket in the centre (widthways) of the inside of the bag, roughly 5 cm beneath the opening edge, and sew into place from the inside – 2–3 mm from the edge of the pocket. This seam will be visible on the outside of the bag, so take care to make sure it is straight and try to complete it without pausing. Check that your thread tension is correct so that the visible seam is as neat as possible.

SEW TOGETHER THE MAIN BODY AND THE END PIECES

Using tailor's chalk, draw a line across one of the end pieces, dividing it into two semi circles. It's now time to sew the end pieces on to the main body of the bag.

Turn the main body inside out, so that the outer pocket is on the inside, and begin pinning the circular end pieces edge to edge with the main body. The main body should wrap around the end pieces perfectly – other than an 18 mm wide gap where the zip will be sewn in.

Position the end piece with the line drawn on it so that the chalk lines up perfectly with the hole for the zip. The purpose of the line on the end piece is to act as a guide when you cut the hole for the zip to be sewn into later.

Sew both end pieces onto the main body, roughly 15 mm from the edge. I find it easiest to have the end pieces lying downwards in the machine, adjusting the main body as you sew. This way, you can make sure that the main body fits the circumference of the circles perfectly, and that there aren't any creases. Sew a few stitches at a time, then adjust the pieces. Sew a little more and repeat. It's trickier than it seems to get it right, so this might take a while.

Next, turn the bag the right way out and cut the end piece along the line you drew – stopping 6 cm before the edge. At the end of the hole, cut two 1 cm snips at a 45 degree angle. Now, firmly press a 1 cm fold inwards along the cut lines. You should also press the small triangular pieces inwards at the end of the cut.

Cut the bag's main zip to a length of 95 cm. Pin the zip (the two pieces together, without a slider) to the opening in the bag, making sure you have a 3 cm overlap inside the bag at each end, and so that the visible section of zip is the same width along its entire length.

Separate the two sides of the zip once it is pinned into place and sew along the length of each half. Begin at the very end by securing the thread, and sew right to the end of the zip and back again. Do the same with the opposite side.

Turn the bag inside out and thread a slider onto each end of the zip, so that it can be opened from both directions.

Turn the bag the right way out and sew vertically across both ends of the zip. Double sew these seams, since they'll be subjected to quite a lot of wear and tear when opening and closing the bag.

BIAS BINDING ON THE INSIDE

Turn the bag inside out. Cut two 105 cm lengths of binding and press them down the middle, lengthways. Next, sew them onto the seams joining the end pieces to the main body of the bag to hide the raw seams.

HANDLES

To sew the handles, you should follow the same instructions as for the firewood holder on page 73, with the difference that there should be 12 cm between the handles on the duffel bag. They should also be positioned so that the distance between the bottom of the handle and the zip seam is 12 cm.

The handles should be secured to the bag with a 20 × 40 mm 'X box' stitch.

TOILETRY BAG

TIME: 4 HOURS | LEVEL 2

A great, simple toiletry bag that borrows its shape from an old Marimekko pouch I've had for years. It doesn't take too long to sew and is easy to adjust to make it your own.

MATERIAL

– densely woven polyester/ cotton canvas outer material, *c.* 30 × 100 cm

– bias binding, 30 mm wide, *c.* 1.5 metres

– cotton/polyester poplin for lining and inner pockets, *c.* 30 × 20 cm

– coil zip with 1 slider, size 5, 30 cm

MEASUREMENTS

– Small: H 15 cm × W 20 cm × D 8 cm

– Large: H 20 cm × W 26 cm × D 10.5 cm

SEW THE SHELL

Cut out the material for the main body of the toiletry bag: 44 × 20 cm for the small version, 59 × 26 cm for the large. Cut out the side pieces: 16 × 10 cm (× 2) or 21 × 13 cm (× 2), respectively. Cut out the lining that will function as the inner pockets of the bag: 37 × 20 cm for the small and 50 × 26 for the large.

Sew a 1 cm wide double folded hem at both short sides of the lining. Place the lining onto the main body; it should be centred, laterally, with the hems upwards. The hems will form the upper edges of the internal pockets. Change to a bobbin thread the same colour as the outer material and an upper thread the same colour as the lining. Sew a vertical row of stitches across the lining to divide it into two pockets on each side.

Draw out the positions for the bottom seams of the lining, *c.* 10 cm for the small bag and 12.5 cm for the larger. Sew these seams.

Cut out two 10 cm lengths of bias binding, press them in the middle and sew them onto the short edges of the side pieces. Pin the first side piece to the main body. It should be centred against the main body, so mark out the middle on both pieces and use that to determine where to pin it. Clip away enough of the seam allowance to enable you to make the corners.

Sew the pieces together *c.* 8–10 mm from the edge. As you approach the bottom where the corner will be sewn, continue straight ahead until 8–10 mm before the bottom edge of the side piece. Lift the presser foot and turn the entire piece 90 degrees. You can now line up the bottom of the side piece with the main body and continue in that new direction. It may be a good idea to have a small pair of pliers or tweezers to hand to pull the material into the right position before you continue. Finish the seam so that the side piece and the main body are joined, and repeat on the opposite side.

ZIP

Cut a length of zip: 28 cm for the small bag, 35 for the larger one. Separate the zip into its two halves; you'll add the slider later. Fold the upper edges of the main body inwards by 1 cm, and press. Sew the two halves of the zip to the upper edges of the bag. Line up one end of the zip with the corner of the bag, leaving you with an excess of 8 cm or 9 cm, respectively, at the other side. For now, don't sew the last 2 cm at the side of the bag with the excess zip.

HANGING HOOK

Cut a length of bias binding: 14 cm for the small bag, 15 cm for the large one. Press in the middle and sew along both sides. Sew this onto the bag at the opposite end to the excess zip. Sew it into the same seam that is holding together the side piece and the main body, c. 15 mm beneath the upper edge of the side piece.

BIAS BINDING

Cut two lengths of binding to sew around the bare seams holding the main body and side pieces together: 48 cm for the small bag, 62 cm for the larger one. Press the binding in the middle.

Begin by sewing the binding on the end of the bag you attached the hanging hook to. Allow the binding to stick up above the zip by c. 2 cm and sew over the edge of the bag. It's tricky to get around the corner and sew the bottom section without the binding bunching up or the lower thread missing the binding (given that you can't see it). So, stop stitching as close to the corner as you can without making a mess. Secure the thread with a quick forward and backstitch. Lift the bag away from the machine, fit the binding around the corner and make a small, 6–7 mm clip on the inside. Carefully glue the binding around the corner (take care to make sure no glue ends up outside the area covered by the binding, as it will be visible) to hold it in place, and begin sewing again, now with the bottom facing upwards. Begin as close to the corner as you can, with a forward and backstitch to secure the thread, and then sew the entire bottom edge and finish off in the same way close to the opposite corner.

Sew this corner in the same way, and finish off at the top, by the other zip. Fold down the excess binding (cut away so that *c.*15 mm excess remains) over the zip and sew it against the edge with 2 parallel seams. Repeat on the other side.

Sew the second piece of binding onto the side where the excess zip is hanging out in the exact same way, but begin by folding a 15 mm hem on the end of the binding tape. Sew this into place over the zip, corner to corner, and down over the edge of the bag. Handle the corners in the same way as before, and finish your seam by folding the bias binding into a hem and sewing it into place on the edge of the bag.

Sew the last piece of zip to the top edge of the bag. Thread the slider onto this so that the bag is open when the slider is at the end with the excess of zip. Cut a 7 cm length of bias binding, press it in the middle (lengthwise) and fold small hems at each end. Place the binding on the length of zip sticking out, and sew it into place with a seam around the edge.

PROJECT COMPONENTS

A Main body, outer material,
   large = 59 × 26 cm,
   small = 44 × 20 cm (× 1)

B Inner pockets, lining,
   large = 50 × 26 cm,
   small = 37 × 20 cm (× 1)

C Side piece, outer material,
   large = 21 × 13 cm,
   small = 16 × 10 cm (× 2)

D Bias binding for main body,
   large = 62 cm × 30 mm,
   small = 48 cm × 30 mm (× 2)

E Bias binding for sides,
   large = 13 cm × 30 mm,
   small = 10 cm × 30 mm (× 2)

F Bias binding hanging hook,
   large = 15 cm × 30 mm,
   small = 14 cm × 30 mm (× 1)

G Zip, size 5, large = 35 cm, small = 28 cm (× 1)

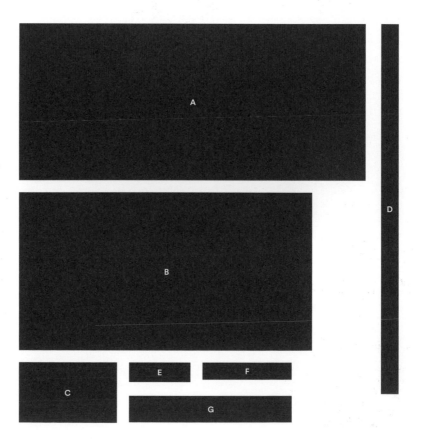

HANGING FLOWERPOT

TIME: 1.5 HOURS | LEVEL 1.5

These hanging flowerpots are made to be hung on the wall or beneath a shelf, and are big enough to hold small herbs or plants. It's easy to adjust the size to the pot you want to use. The hangers need an inner pot, ideally one without any holes in the bottom, to collect any run off water. I bought a few pots and bowls I thought were the right size from charity shops, and based the hangers on those.

WORK OUT THE SIZE OF THE PIECES

The hangers take the shape of an open-ended cuboid, and are sewn with a main body (which functions as two sides and the bottom of the pot) and two side pieces equal in width to the main body, leaving you with a square opening at the top. If you have an inner pot with a diameter of 12 cm (like the pot containing the parsley in the image), the circumference of your hanger needs to be 13.5 × 3.14 = 42 cm, to avoid being too small.

Divide the circumference by the 4 pieces (42 / 4 = 10.5) and add a 1 cm seam allowance to each side (10.5 + 1 + 1 = 12.5). That means 12.5 cm wide pieces for a circumference of 42 cm.

Let's imagine that your pot is 10 cm high; that means a height of 11 cm should be sufficient for your hanger. The length of the main body should be at least the height × 2 + bottom + hems at top (11 × 2 + 12.5 + 2.5 = 37 cm) and the side pieces should equal the height + seam allowance + hems (11 + 1.5 + 2.5 = 15 cm).

Cut out a main body measuring 12.5 × 37 cm and two side pieces measuring 12.5 × 15 cm. For the side pieces, you should give the corners a slight curve, something like a 2 cm radius, at one end of the 12.5 cm sides, and cut the corners so that they are rounded.

MATERIAL

- densely woven polyester/cotton canvas outer material, c. 30 × 100 cm
- leather, 2 mm thickness, 12 × 12 mm
- leather strap, 2 mm thickness, c. 50 cm × 10 mm
- rivets, 6 mm (× 2)

105

Fit the pieces together so that the side pieces are precisely lined up with the middle of the main body. Do this by marking out the mid-point on both pieces, then pinning them together.

Begin sewing from the middle of the bottom, outwards, and keep an 8–10 mm distance from the edge. Sew with an 8–10 mm seam allowance, in other words. When you reach the corner, sew one stitch at a time, and turn the main body slightly in relation to the side piece after each stitch. Doing so will help to produce several small creases (which are inevitable, since the material has no give whatsoever) rather than one large one. Continue sewing stitch by stitch along the curve, and then straighten up again. Sew both seams in the same way.

Trim the upper edge so that it is the same height all the way round, then fold it inwards and sew a c.15 mm hem. Press the seam allowance apart at the corners so that the material isn't too thick to sew.

LEATHER STRAPS

Cut a 10 mm width of leather strap to the required length and round the corners. Position the end of the strap in the middle of one side of the hanger, and use a hole punch to make a hole through both the strap and the main body of the hanger.

Cut out 2 leather pieces measuring 12 × 12 mm to rivet the strap against.

Make a hole in the middle of each piece, and rivet the first to the leather strap and the hanger; the small piece of leather should be on the inside of the pot. Now do the same with the other side. If you really want to make the hanger look smart, you can also sew bias binding around the open seams inside.

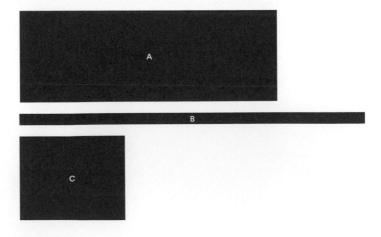

PROJECT COMPONENTS

A Main body, outer
   material, 37 × 12.5 cm
   (× 1)

B Leather strap, 2 mm,
   50 cm × 10 mm (× 1)

C Side piece, outer
   material, 12.5 × 15 cm
   (× 2)

107

FRUIT BOWL

TIME: 1.5 HOURS | LEVEL 1.5

This fruit bowl is a variation on the flowerpot hanger, sewn as an open cylinder instead of a cuboid. You can hang it on the wall or place it on the table as a kind of fruit bowl bag. Naturally, you could also make small, cylindrical pot hangers if you like.

MEASURE OUT THE PIECES

Find a suitable plate with a diameter of 18–24 cm. I found one that wasn't a perfect circle, but somewhere between square and round, and thought that might work.

Measure the circumference of your plate and cut out a rectangular piece of material the same length as this, plus 2 cm. The width should be c.20–25 cm.

Draw around the plate onto the material and cut out a circular piece of material the exact same size as the plate.

SEW THE SHELL TOGETHER

Sew the pieces together a few stitches at a time. This will allow you to turn the main body at small increments, following the curve of the bottom without causing creases. Don't sew the first 5 cm of fabric, and continue until there is roughly 5 cm remaining at the other end.

Sew together the two ends of the main body at the right point to be able to complete the seam with the bottom.

Cut away any excess from the main body so that you are left with a 1 cm hem. Press a c.20 cm length of bias binding and sew it onto this hem.

Finish off the bottom seam. Fold the bias binding you sewed onto the seam of the main body to one side and sew over it.

MATERIAL
- densely-woven polyester/ cotton canvas outer material, c.30 × 100 cm
- rivets, 6 mm (× 2)
- pieces of leather, c.15 × 15 mm (× 2)
- leather strap, 2 mm thickness, c.50 × 10 mm

Fold down the top of the bowl to the height you want it, in a thick double hem, then sew around the bottom edge of this hem.

Cut out a *c.*62 cm length of bias binding and press it in the middle. Sew this binding around the bottom seam after you trim it to a reasonable height of 1 cm.

LEATHER HANDLES

Cut out the leather strap and the smaller pieces of leather, and round off all of the corners.

Punch holes in the middle of each piece using a hole punch.

Hold the strap in place in the centre. It should be in such a position that it can be neatly folded down to one side, over the edge of the bowl. Next, use the hole punch to make holes in both the bowl and the strap. Rivet the small pieces of leather to the inside and the strap to the outside of the bowl. Only hammer the rivet in half way so that you can still turn the handle. This way, you can use the handle if you want to hang it up, or fold it down if you want your fruit bowl on the table.

PROJECT COMPONENTS

A Main body, outer
   material, 65 × 24 cm
   (× 1)

B Bottom, outer material,
   20 cm diameter (× 1)

C Leather strap,
   2 mm thickness,
   35 cm × 15 mm (× 1)

D Leather for reverse of
   rivets, 2 mm thickness,
   15 × 15 mm (× 2)

SMALL BACKPACK

TIME: 8 HOURS | LEVEL 3.5

This backpack has an asymmetrical design and is made up of irregular pieces, both of which make it slightly challenging – primarily to construct, but also to sew. It's a case of making the pieces fit together in the end, and for the shape to be nice and even. The backpack is just big enough to hold a thin 13" laptop, and it fits your back like a glove. It's also a great bag for running.

CUT OUT ACCORDING TO PATTERN

Make paper patterns or measure and draw directly onto the material, following the outlines of the project components on p. 114. All measurements are in cm and include seam allowances. Cut out the pieces.

SEW TOGETHER THE FRONT AND SIDES, AND SEW THE FRONT INNER POCKET

Cut out a piece of lining; it should follow the same angles as the front piece, but it should measure 23 cm along the bottom edge, 18 cm along the top, and should have a height of 19 cm.

MATERIAL

– densely woven polyester/ cotton canvas outer material, c. 50 × 100 cm
– cotton/polyester poplin lining, c. 40 × 50 cm
– polyester webbing strap, 20 mm width, 1.5 m
– strap adjusters, 20 mm (× 2)
– coil zip with two sliders, size 5, 50 cm

Fold and press a 2 cm hem at the top of the lining, and sew along both the upper and lower edge of this hem. Fold and press 1.5 cm of material at the bottom of the lining. This time, fold in the opposite direction (inwards).

Place the piece of lining on top of the front piece so that the top hem (turned outwards) is 4 cm beneath the upper edge of the front piece – the shorter of the two short sides.

Press in the edges of the front piece 1 cm over the lining. Position the side pieces so that they overlap the folded front piece by 1 cm.

Pin and sew together with a seam from the outside, c. 2 mm from the edge and with another, parallel seam 8 mm away. Both should be sewn

PROJECT COMPONENTS

A Back section, outer
   material
B Lid, outer material
C Bottom, outer material
D Front, outer material
E Sides, outer material
   (× 2)
F Shoulder straps, outer
   material (× 4)
G Adjustable straps
   for shoulderstraps,
   polyester webbing,
   50 cm × 20 mm (× 2)
H Front inner pocket,
   lining (× 1)
I Zip, size 5, 46 cm (× 1)
J Shoulder strap triangles,
   outer material, (× 2)
K Computer pocket at
   back, lining, (× 1)
L Carry handle, polyester
   webbing, 20 cm ×
   20 mm (× 1)

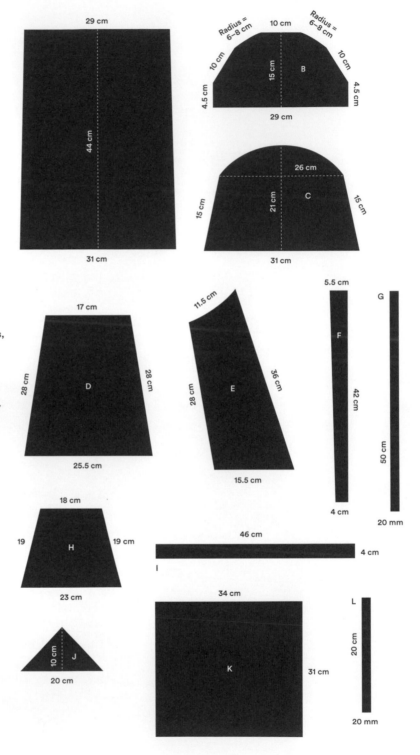

with the front piece facing upwards so that the more attractive upper thread will be visible from the outside. Since these seams will be visible on the front of the backpack, take care to work in a straight line. I tend to use the edge of the fabric as a guide, picking a point on the presser foot to follow this line. Then, while I'm sewing, I focus on that point, rather than on the needle. It might sound banal, but when you're working with slightly thicker materials, you might find that your machine likes to go off to one side, which means you need to give it your full attention and steer the material carefully if you want to end up with straight seams. Repeat with the other side.

Next, sew the rows of stitches that will form the bottom of the internal pocket. Place the material front side up (so that the more attractive upper thread stitches are visible on the outside of the bag), and feel for the point where the pocket begins – i.e. where material gets thicker. Draw a line along this edge, and sew with the outside of the bag facing up, *c.*5 mm above the line. Begin where the vertical stitches (attaching the side pieces) meet the line using a forward and backstitch, and finish off in the same way at the other end. Next, sew a second, parallel seam.

SEW THE ZIP TO THE FRONT

Cut a 46 cm length of zip, but don't thread a slider onto it.

Press a 1 cm fold along the top edge of the front piece and sides. Clip the fold in a few places so that the fabric lies flat, despite the curve.

Mark out the mid-point of the front piece and the zip, line them up with one another, and use a pin to hold them in place.

Sew the zip into place on the front of the bag. I find it easier to sew without any pins – i.e. to adjust the position of the zip by hand, sewing a few stitches at a time before turning, adjusting, and sewing some more. Stretch out the zip as you sew so that it is at its full length. This means the zip will be angled slightly inwards later.

SEW TOGETHER THE BOTTOM, FRONT AND COMPUTER POCKET

Cut out a piece of lining measuring *c.*34 × 31 cm. This will form the computer pocket at the back of the bag.

Fold and press a 2 cm double hem at the top, then sew a row of stitches along its upper and lower edges.

Bring together the front piece, back piece and computer pocket as follows: place the back piece on top of the bottom piece, so that its lower edge is lined up with the edge of the bottom piece. Next, place the back pocket on top of the back piece with the 'front' of the pocket facing upwards – i.e. with the hem visible.

Push two pins into the back piece and pocket to hold them in position, then sew a seam 1 cm from the edge, through all three layers.

Next, take the finished front piece (including the sides) and mark the mid-point of its bottom edge. Line up this point with the mid-point of the bottom piece (right side to right side), and sew together with a 1 cm seam allowance. It's easiest to begin in the middle and sew one half first, followed by the other – working from the middle out.

SEW THE LID AND ZIP

Take the piece of material for the lid and press a 1 cm fold around the rounded side.

Clip the fold in places so that the hem curves nicely.

Now, sew the other side of the zip that you already attached to the front piece along the entire edge of the lid. Before you begin, mark out the mid-point of both the zip and the lid, line these up with one another and pin into place. You should have an equal amount of excess zip on both sides of the lid. Sew one stitch at a time, and stretch out the zip as you sew. If you prefer, you can separate the zip into two pieces and join them together again later, when you add the slider ahead of sewing the side seams.

SHOULDER STRAP TRIANGLES, SHOULDER STRAPS AND CARRY HANDLE

Cut out two isosceles triangles measuring 20 cm at their base, and 10 cm high.

Fold in half, then fold a c. 1 cm seam allowance on both the top and bottom sides, and press.

Trim away the fold in the c. 1.5 cm closest to the base of the triangle on both sides. This is to avoid having too many layers to sew through when the triangles are later sewn into the side seams of the bag.

Place a 50 cm length of polyester webbing inside the triangles. The end of the webbing should sit at the point of the triangle, and it should be sewn into place with a row of stitching along the outer edge of the triangle.

Sew around the edge, and sew an extra seam along the inner edge of the webbing strap as reinforcement.

Take the pieces of fabric you cut out for the shoulder straps and fold and press 1 cm of fabric along the long sides of all four pieces.

Place two of these pieces on top of one another with the folds inside, and sew together with a seam along both long sides, 3 mm from the edge.

Thread a strap adjuster onto the thin end of each shoulder strap. Next, fold back around 5 cm at the end of the strap that is threaded through the strap adjuster, and make sure it is centred.

Sew the end of the strap back against the main strap using a 2 × 3 square of stitching. The folded side of the strap should be on the inside when the backpack is being worn, so make sure that the strap adjusters are facing the right way.

Next, cut a 20 cm length of polyester webbing, fold it down the middle and sew a 10 cm seam down the middle of the folded strap. You should be left with 5 cm of free strap at each end.

Thread a slider onto the zip and close it as far as you can – but only so far that you can still manage to sew the side seams.

SEW TOGETHER THE SIDES

Pin the side pieces to the back piece (with the computer pocket smooth and in the right position, flat against the back), and pin the shoulder strap triangles into place at the bottom edge, where the sides meet the bottom.

Sew everything together. Begin at the bottom, and sew until you have passed over the zip. Sew back across the zip, then again, until you reach the edge of the lid before its straight side. Stop there and secure the thread.

You can now turn the bag the right way out, push the shoulder straps into place beneath the top edge of the back piece and test out the angle and distance between them, to see what suits you. Roughly 5–7 cm between the straps, angled slightly outwards, tends to work best.

Mark the right position and turn the backpack inside out again. Use your markings to pin the shoulder straps into place. The ends of the straps should sit edge to edge with the lid. Next, pin the carry handle into place between the straps. Sew the top seam by folding the back piece c. 12 mm over both the lid and shoulder straps; your entire seam should be 10 mm from the edge. Sew this seam twice to give it reinforcement. Now all that remains to finish off the bag is to sew bias binding around the inside seams.

DESIGNING YOUR OWN PROJECTS

Once you've completed one or two of the projects in this book, you'll likely be comfortable enough to start coming up with designs of your own. When you first start sewing, you'll probably notice that you automatically start paying more attention to how material objects are made – examining how the pieces are sewn together, checking what kind of seams have been used, feeling the quality of the material. Looking for interesting solutions and checking the construction of various bags and objects can be a pretty enlightening process. It makes you think about which aspects or ideas you might borrow for your own projects. You'll also start seeking out useful materials when the opportunity arises; saving suitable remnants and taking buckles and other useful attachments from things when they break.

So, what might you come up with for your own projects? I tend to take my everyday needs as a starting point. When I'm in the mood for sewing, my to-do list contains, among other things, a good number of storage solutions – a nice hanging shoe rack, for example, with pockets for shoes; something which can be hung up among the coats in the hallway to save space. I've also been thinking about hanging 'buckets', similar in shape to the fruit basket from this book, but bigger, for all those gloves, hats and scarves. I've actually also been meaning to sew a sturdy pair of mittens with a removable lining made from felted wool. A pair of slippers with a felt sole and an upper made from fabric or leather would also be fun to try, as would a pair of bare-foot shoes with a simple rubber sole and leather upper. But first: I need to make a hard case for my new spinning reel. I was planning to get hold of a suitable cardboard tube for the project, then sewing a fabric tube with a zip opening at the top, which can be pulled onto and glued to the tube. But that will have to wait until I've mended the children's ripped trousers piled up by the sewing machine.

Once you start thinking and looking around, you'll find ideas for a range of different projects. Using something that you have designed, measured and made into a pattern, cut out and sewn together gives a certain kind of satisfaction that you'll remember for a long time whenever you use your object. Good luck!

Thanks Mum, for always letting me borrow your sewing machine when I was a teenager, despite your misgivings. I was glad to see this week that you are still using it.

Heavy-Duty Sewing
Text © 2016 Anton Sandqvist

Published in 2018 by Frances Lincoln,
an imprint of The Quarto Group
The Old Brewery, 6 Blundell Street,
London N7 9BH, United Kingdom
T (0)20 7700 6700 F (0)20 7700 8066
www.QuartoKnows.com

First published in 2016 by Natur & Kultur, Stockholm
Photography by Knotan Tobias Arnerlöv
Designed by Sebastian Wadsted
Edited by Maria Nilsson & Russell Walls
Translated by Alice Menzies

A catalogue record for this book is available for the British Library.

ISBN 978 0 7112 3925 8

Printed and bound in China

9 8 7 6 5 4 3 2

Brimming with creative inspiration, how-to projects and useful information to enrich your everyday life, Quarto Knows is a favourite destination for those pursuing their interests and passions. Visit our site and dig deeper with our books into your area of interest: Quarto Creates, Quarto Cooks, Quarto Homes, Quarto Lives, Quarto Drives, Quarto Explores, Quarto Gifts, or Quarto Kids.

FSC
www.fsc.org
MIX
Paper from
responsible sources
FSC® C104723